For Peter
With love from

Grace Walker
St. Valentine's Day
14 February 2022

to

Grace

with all best wishes

John
_____

1ˢᵗ Nov. '02

# $\mathcal{P}$EOPLE
## MY
## TEACHERS

The author in Pembrokeshire, Wales.

*Around the world in eighty years*

Distributed by STL, PO Box 300,
Carlisle, Cumbria CA3 0QS
Worldwide coedition organized and
produced by
Angus Hudson Ltd,
Concorde House, Grenville Place,
Mill Hill, London NW7 3SA, England
Tel: +44 (0)20 8959 3668
Fax: +44 (0)20 8959 3678

Printed in Singapore

*Overall:* **Skomer and Gateholm islands from the Pembrokeshire mainland.**

*All the royalties from this book
have been irrevocably assigned
to the Evangelical Literature Trust (UK),
which distributes books to pastors,
theological teachers and students,
and seminary libraries, in the developing world.*

*Further information may be obtained from,
and donations sent to:*
*The Evangelical Literature Trust*
*The Church Office*
*Stoke Park Drive,*
*Ipswich IP2 9TH*
*United Kingdom*

# PEOPLE
## MY
## TEACHERS

# JOHN STOTT

*with photographs by the author*

CANDLE
BOOKS

# Preface

Two or three years ago I thought of calling this book *Around the World in Eighty Years* – echoing the title of Jules Verne's novel, *Around the World in Eighty Days* – since in 2001 I celebrated my 80th birthday and during my lifetime I have been privileged to travel all over the world. But no sooner had this idea formulated in my mind than I discovered that two other authors had already laid claim to this title. In consequence, the main title is now *People My Teachers*. This indicates that it is a companion volume to *The Birds Our Teachers* (1999), except that now our teachers are humans not birds.

What I have done is draw an imaginary circle round the globe, and plot sixteen stopping places on it, at each of which I pause to introduce somebody to you. The sixteen people I introduce all share four characteristics.

First, they are all historical people, who have lived. Some lived in the distant past, like the apostle Paul and Saint David of Wales. Others have lived and worked in the recent past, like Festo Kivengere of Uganda and Richard Wurmbrand of Romania. None of them is still alive today, although I attempt to bring them alive again by re-telling their story.

Secondly, each of them is associated with a particular place, in geography as well as history, so that I try to set each person in his or her context.

Thirdly, each has had a distinguished career, from which we are still able to learn today.

Fourthly, I have had a personal link of some kind with each of them. Some I have known personally, like Dr Paul White and Bishop Bjørn Bue. In other cases I have visited their grave, like Shackleton's on South Georgia and Temple Gairdner's in Cairo. Yet others have made an impact on my life either by a book they have written or by their reputation. In one or other of these ways I have been able to share a personal anecdote about each.

Thus history and geography, biography (theirs) and autobiography (mine) combine to fashion each story that I tell. Photography is perhaps a fifth factor, because I am able to share with my readers a number of my own pictures. The only absent characteristic is chronology, for as we pursue our journey round the world we will follow a geographical but not a chronological order.

All my sixteen people have been leaders, and most have been Christian leaders. But some have had only a loose connection with the Christian community (like Darwin and Shackleton). Only one (Gandhi) was not a Christian, although at one point in his life he nearly became one. All of them have a lesson or lessons to teach us.

I gratefully acknowledge the help I have received in producing this book. I begin with Tim Dowley and Peter Wyart of Three's Company, whose design skills I greatly admire. Next, I am grateful to the relatives and friends of some of my characters, like Bishop Bjørn Bue's widow and his episcopal successor, and Dr Paul White's widow Ruth. Several organisations have given me help: The College of Arms, the Nepali Christian Fellowship, the South American Missionary Society and the Overseas Missionary Fellowship.

**The cliffs of Skokholm island, Pembrokeshire, West Wales.**

**The happy triumvirate: Frances Whitehead, John Stott and Corey Widmer.**

In particular, my secretary Frances Whitehead and my study assistant Corey Widmer have given me much assistance. We work well together as a team, and call ourselves 'the happy triumvirate'. I am deeply grateful to them both.

*John Stott*
New Year, 2002

# Contents

# 1. David

## *Patron saint of Wales*

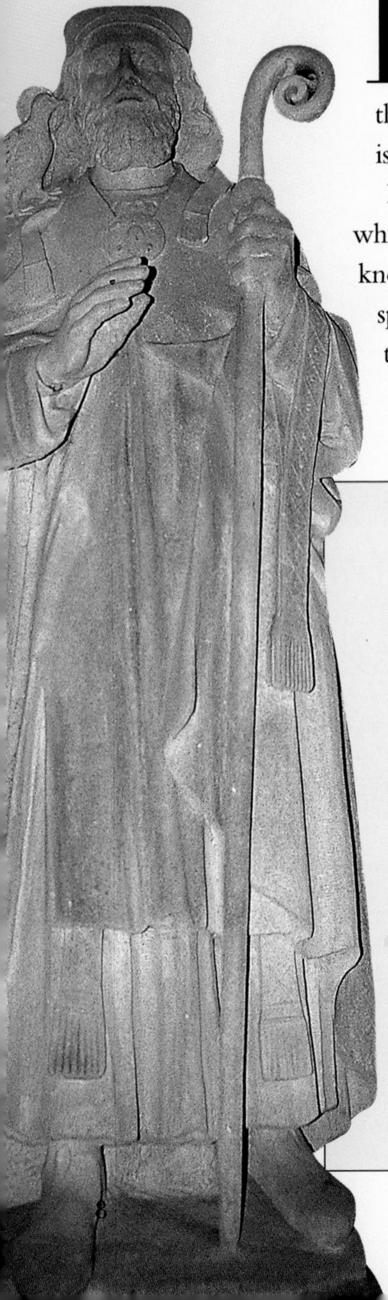

Sculpture of St David in St David's Cathedral, Pembrokeshire.

I FIRST VISITED WEST WALES FIFTY YEARS AGO, and soon afterwards bought The Hookses, a disused and somewhat derelict farmhouse with its outbuildings. Situated on the coast a mile outside the village of Dale in Pembrokeshire, it nestles among the cliffs, and is protected from every direction except the south.

In southerly gales, however, horizontal rain is driven up the valley, while huge Atlantic rollers come crashing onto the cliffs below. I have known the whole terrain whiten, not from frost or snow but from spume blown up from the surface of the sea. Then the salt turns the bracken brown. From my study window I look out across West Dale Bay to the open ocean beyond. I sometimes claim to have an uninterrupted view of the South Pole!

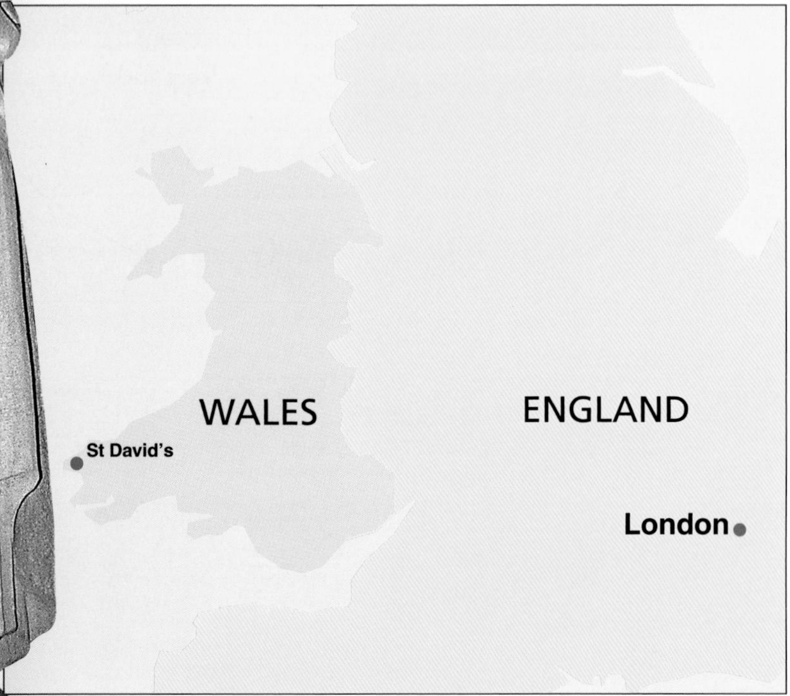
WALES
ENGLAND
St David's
London

**The Hookses, Dale, Pembrokeshire, West Wales.**

As an adopted son of Wales (when not at The Hookses or travelling I live in London), I have naturally taken a keen interest in Welsh history and culture, even though the southern half of Pembrokeshire is known as 'little England beyond Wales', being English– not Welsh-speaking.

It is not known how or when the gospel of Jesus Christ first reached Britain. Presumably it was brought by Christian legionaries in the Roman army of occupation, or by traders, as early as the first or second century. We also celebrate St Alban as the first known British martyr, who probably lost his life during the persecution associated with either the emperor Decius (AD 250) or the emperor Valerian (AD 257-8). What is evident is that the church was sufficiently well organized by AD 314 to send three bishops (of London, York and Lincoln) to the first Synod of Arles in south-east France.

This early British church is usually called the 'Celtic Church' because it was indigenous to Wales, Scotland, Ireland and Brittany and because it asserted its independence of Rome. Not until the arrival of Augustine of Canterbury (597) and the Synod of Whitby (663-4) did the Celtic Church submit to the authority of Rome.

Before and after this, however, during the whole period between the fourth and the twelfth centuries, the Celtic Church manifested considerable vitality.

In recent years there has been in the west a growing fascination with

**St David's Cathedral, Pembrokeshire.**

all things deemed 'Celtic', and especially with so-called Celtic 'spirituality'. Nevertheless, there is neither certainty nor agreement among scholars whether there ever has been a coherent Celtic spirituality, and if so what its chief ingredients were. Some have a romantic vision of feminism, environmentalism and mysticism as constituting its essence, while others reject its Christian basis altogether in favour of New Age thought.

A more moderate view begins with the recognition that the Celtic church shared with the Catholic church the fundamentals of the Christian faith: the authority of the Bible, the doctrine of the Trinity, the belief that God is both transcendent (as Creator, Lord and Judge) and immanent (near and accessible to his people), and the centrality of the cross. These truths may be termed 'Celtic', but they are by no means exclusively so.

At the same time, there are certain emphases which, though common to all believers, may be claimed as specially emphasized by Celtic Christians.

(1) *Closeness to Creation.* Celtic Christians acknowledged that God is the creator and sustainer of all things, so that 'the earth is the Lord's, and everything in it' (Ps. 24:1). They worshipped the Creator but did not confuse him with his creation.

(2) *Practising the Presence of God.* Because the Celts believed in the pervasive presence of God, they were notable for the scope of their prayers. 'They cover every aspect of life from cradle to grave, from rising to going to sleep, from milking the cow to laying the fire'.[1]

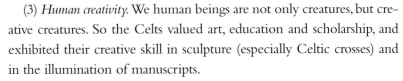

**Puffin in Pembrokeshire.**

**A carved Celtic cross outside the parish church, Nevern, Pembrokeshire.**

(3) *Human creativity.* We human beings are not only creatures, but creative creatures. So the Celts valued art, education and scholarship, and exhibited their creative skill in sculpture (especially Celtic crosses) and in the illumination of manuscripts.

(4) *A simple lifestyle.* It is natural, because of their view of creation, that the Celts received God's gifts with gratitude. But simplicity sometimes degenerated into an extreme austerity.

(5) *Enthusiasm for mission.* The great Celtic names (Patrick, Aidan, Columba, David and others) were great missionaries. The early Celtic church also sent out many Christian evangelists, whose names are not known, to Scotland, France, Switzerland and Northern Italy.

It was during the early Celtic period that David (Dewi), who is now the patron saint of Wales, came into prominence. Unfortunately no reliable biography of him has ever been written, so that his story is a mixture of history and legend. Nevertheless we can affirm some things about him with a measure of confidence. He was born about 520 into a noble family in south-west Wales, and after his ordination he founded a number of churches and monasteries. He himself settled in the church and monastery at Mynyw (in Latin Menevia), which is now St David's. As a scholar he built up an extensive library, although it was later destroyed by the Vikings. It is claimed that he made a pilgrimage to Jerusalem, where he was made a bishop. Then in AD 545 at the Council of Brefi (now Llanddewi Brefi) he was acknowledged primate of Wales. But little credence can be given to the story that, while he was speaking at the council, the ground on which he was standing miraculously rose up, so that everybody could see and hear him.

St David's Cathedral is a worthy monument to David. It claims to preserve his bones, and two visits to his relics were deemed equivalent to a single pilgrimage to Rome. In fact, the present cathedral is the fourth church to have been erected on the same site. The first is said to have been built by David himself, but it was burned down in 645. The second and third buildings, hiding like the first in the valley of the little river Alun, and with a stunted tower designed to escape the notice of marauding Danes, were nevertheless sacked by them in 1078 and 1088. It is the

**Sculpted head outside St David's Cathedral.**

fourth which is substantially the present cathedral; it was constructed by the Normans beginning in 1180.

The cathedral is built of purplish Cambrian sandstone from nearby seacliff quarries. Its exterior is plain, even austere, but its interior has been decorated by successive generations, especially by Bishop Henry Gower (1328-47). He also finished the construction of the Bishop's Palace (as much for visiting pilgrims as for himself and his own retinue). Its magnificent ruins draw many tourists today. The cathedral was restored by Gilbert Scott in the 1860s.

I have often wondered how much David knew and appreciated the wildlife for which Pembrokeshire is famous, especially its birds. Is it significant that, according to legend, while he was addressing the Council of Brefi, a white dove flew to him and perched on his right shoulder? Consequently, the modern stone figure of David in the cathedral depicts him with a dove on his right shoulder. Less encouraging is 'the fable fathered upon St David', which George Owen recorded in his *Description of Pembrokeshire* (1603). 'Being seriouse occupied in the night tyme in his divine orizons' (prayers), David was so distracted by 'the sweete tuninges of the Nightingall' that he found himself unable to concentrate. He could not 'fasten his minde upon heavenlie cogitacions'. So he prayed 'that from that tyme forward there might never a Nightingall sing within his dioces', which (according to this fable) 'was

**The tower of St David's Cathedral can be seen over the walls of the ruined Bishop's Palace.**

**A Nightingale in full-throated song in April in Kent, south-east England.**

**A carved representation of a coracle on a choir seat in St David's Cathedral.**

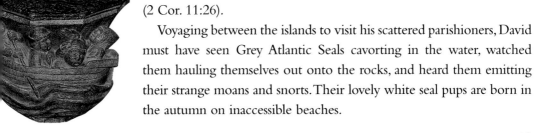

the cause of confininge of the bird out of this Countrey . . . '.[2]

The Pembrokeshire coast was probably forested in David's day, but the offshore islands, specially Skomer and Skokholm, windswept and treeless, will have been covered in the spring (as they are now) with a spectacular red, white and blue carpet of red campions, sea campions and bluebells. David must have been familiar with the islands. The larger ones were inhabited and farmed in his day, and signs of their ancient hut circles can still be seen. St David's Head is the most westerly point of the Welsh mainland and is surrounded by sea; the cathedral is only half a mile from the sea to the south. St David's was also on the regular sea route between north-western Europe and southern Ireland. So traders and missionaries will have travelled that way in both directions. Their precarious vessels may have been 'coracles' (Welsh) or 'curraghs' (Irish), which Ronald Lockley described as 'saucer-like, waterproofed, lath-and-hide canoes'.[3] Flat-bottomed, with no keel, and only a single sail, 'like a fleet-toed dancer the curragh skimmed over the white breaking currents, a living bird of the waves . . . '.[4] If this was his mode of travel, David, like the apostle Paul, must frequently have been 'in danger at sea' (2 Cor. 11:26).

Voyaging between the islands to visit his scattered parishioners, David must have seen Grey Atlantic Seals cavorting in the water, watched them hauling themselves out onto the rocks, and heard them emitting their strange moans and snorts. Their lovely white seal pups are born in the autumn on inaccessible beaches.

We cannot be sure that the breeding habits of local seabirds were the same in David's day as they are today, but I guess they were not very different. We certainly marvel today at the 30,000 or so pairs of Gannets, which occupy the whole of the north-western corner of Grassholm; at the tens of thousands of Puffins and Manx Shearwaters which lay their single egg in the burrows under our feet on Skomer and Skokholm; and at the Fulmars, Kittiwakes, Guillemots and Razorbills which occupy the perilous cliff ledges at different levels.

I have no wish to add to the mythology of St David by depicting him as a Celtic St Francis. But I feel confident that, if David had lived in our century, he would have wanted to celebrate nature's biodiversity as we do. The birds of the Pembrokeshire islands spend most of their lives out in the open ocean. They come to land only for the three or four months of the breeding season. It is then that they are most vulnerable, and it is our responsibility to protect them.

*Top:* **Bluebells and Red Campions on Skomer Island.**

*Above:* **Another view of St David's Cathedral.**

FOOTNOTES

1. Elizabeth Culling, *What is Celtic Christianity?* (Grove Books revised edition, 1994), p. 18.
2. Quoted by R. M. Lockley in *Pembrokeshire* (Robert Hale, London 1957), p. 142.
3. *Ibid*, p. 26
4. R. M. Lockley, *The Seals and the Curragh* (J. M. Dent, 1954), pp. 8, 9.

# Wildlife of the Pembrokeshire coast

*Overall*: **West Dale Bay, Pembrokeshire in a south-easterly gale.**
*Inset left*: **Lesser Black-backed Gulls nesting among bluebells on Skokholm Island.**
*Inset right*: **Grey Atlantic Seal pup.**

# 2. Bjørn Bue

## *Lutheran bishop of Stavanger, Norway*

ONE CANNOT VISIT SCANDINAVIA WITHOUT thinking of the Vikings. They dominated much of Europe during the ninth and tenth centuries. Children have always been fascinated by their colourful names like Godfred Fairhair, Harold Bluetooth, Svein Forkbeard and of course the fabled Danish King Knut (Canute).

The so-called 'Viking Age' lasted for 300 years, from about 770 to 1070. They sailed in their sturdy oak long boats, by the power of wind and oar, along the coasts of Germany, Holland, France, Spain and Italy, and up their rivers. They penetrated east as far as Constantinople and west across the North Atlantic even to Labrador. They also sailed round the Orkneys and the Shetlands and down the Irish Sea, raiding unprotected inlets in Scotland, Ireland and Wales. Traces of Viking influence remain today in the names they gave such islands as Gateholm, Skokholm, and Grassholm, since 'holm' is the Danish word for a small island.

Wherever they went, they spread rape, pillage, murder and destruction. It is not an accident that 'viking' means 'warrior' or

'pirate'. In the choir vestry of St David's Cathedral a wooden plaque lists all the Bishops of St David's, going right back to David himself, and against 5 or 6 of them is written the one word 'Slain'. No wonder some western litanies at that time included the petition 'From the fury of the Norsemen, O Lord, deliver us'.

Yet the Vikings have been to some degree maligned. Their bad reputation was given them by their victims' hostile chronicles; it could hardly be called impartial. The fact is that the Vikings were not motivated only by greed and cruelty. The basic impulse behind their raids, according to Dr Gwyn Jones, was 'recurrent over-population and land shortage'. In his definitive work *A History of the Vikings* he continues:

> *The deeper causes of the Viking movement overseas were rooted in human nature: the northern peoples had needs and ambitions, were prepared to make demands, and had the will, strength and technical means to enforce them. They wanted land to farm, wealth to make life splendid, or bearable, and some of them wanted dignity and fame. Trade, colonization, piracy and war would get them these things . . .*[1]

**A reconstructed Viking longship.**

**The Revd. Dr. Vidar Haanes at the Thingvellir, or Field of Assembly, site of the Icelandic 'Althing', possibly the world's oldest parliament.**

More simply, Dr Gwyn Jones wrote:

*they were neither super-human nor sub-human; but precisely and generically human – in their greed, treachery, cruelty and violence, as in their energy, generosity, loyalty and familial kindness, and recognizably one and the same species as their neighbours . . .*[2]

These Viking explorers and colonizers also left behind them a variety of blessings. One was an early form of democracy, the 'Thing' which is the Old Norse word for a public assembly of free men, both chiefs and people. They met to debate items of regional or national concern. They elected their own president or 'lawspeaker', who was the guardian of the constitution and of human rights.

Perhaps the best example is Thingvellir (literally 'the field of assembly') in Iceland which I visited in 1988. It is the impressive site of the 'Althing', which claims to have been the world's oldest parliament. It had two chambers. It first met in the year 930. In 1000 it voted for Iceland to become Christian. Greenland followed, and later still Norway and Sweden. (Denmark had already embraced the gospel.) The Althing continued to meet until Iceland submitted to Norwegian rule in 1262.

All this is of personal interest to me because the Stotts appear to be descended from the Vikings. In Old English, according to the dictionaries, a 'stot' was either a horse or a young bull or indeed 'a stupid, clumsy person'. As an intransitive verb 'to stot' means to jump or spring. It is still used in South Africa of some antelopes which are said to be 'stotting' when they 'make short high jumps' (all four feet at a time), especially 'as a defensive or warning action'. In the North of England, however, a 'stotty cake' is a kind of coarse bread made from white dough.

One wonders whether these picturesque meanings of 'Stot' or 'Stott' were an allusion to aspects of our character. Were we (are we?) as stubborn or clumsy as a bull, as sprightly as an antelope or as thick as dough? I prefer to think that our Viking ancestors were not so much bullish in character, as cattle breeders, who settled somewhere on the coast of England or Scotland.[3]

At all events, whenever I have visited Scandinavia, I have told my hosts of my Viking origins, and have asked them to receive me not as an alien but as a lost son who has come home!

There is another link between Norway and England, of which I enjoy reminding my Norwegian friends, namely that while Norsemen were plundering England, the English were evangelizing Norway. True, the first Scandinavian converts had been won by Anskar (801-865), 'the apostle of the north'. But it was King Olaf Tryggvasson and King Olaf Haraldsson, both originally Viking chiefs, who after their conversion at the beginning of the eleventh century invited English clergy to evangelize and teach their people. Canute (Knut, 1016-1035), King of

**Norwegian fjord.**

England and Denmark (which then included Norway), completed the process of Christianizing Norway. Consequently, Professor Kenneth Scott Latourette could write: 'The Church in Norway was the offspring of the English church'.[4]

One of my visits to Norway took place in May 1986. I was the guest of Bjørn Bue, who had just been consecrated Lutheran Bishop of Stavanger on Norway's south-western coast. Let me tell you something about him.

Having graduated at the Free Faculty of Theology in Oslo, Bjørn Bue spent nineteen years as a missionary in French-speaking Cameroon, West Africa. Here he gained the nickname 'potato pastor' on account of his concern to improve local agriculture. When he returned to Norway, he became involved in both student work and parish work, before becoming Bishop. Outside his diocesan responsibilities he was strongly committed to mission. He longed that Norway would be re-evangelized, and that the church would develop new ways to reach the unreached and to penetrate secular society for Christ. He was also committed to justice for the oppressed, understanding for immigrants and the care of the environment. He was described after his death as 'the most dynamic and warm-hearted bishop in Norway', whose heart was 'brimming with love for the suffering'.[5]

**A little Lutheran church in Iceland.**

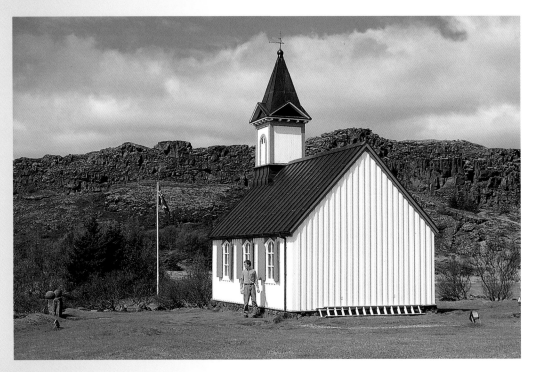

Stavanger Cathedral, Norway.

Bishop Bjørn and I had been friends for some years, especially through our common participation in the Lausanne movement for world mission. He had brought a group of Norwegian pastors to the UK to see the work of our London Institute for Contemporary Christianity. Now he had kindly invited me to pay a return visit, in order to address his clergy. We had gathered in Stavanger Cathedral (with its massive Norman pillars dating from the twelfth century) for the final service on the Friday evening.

The service was almost over. I had finished my sermon, having preached from the magnificent baroque pulpit, and been interpreted by Dean Enok Aadnoy, and had now taken my place next to him in the chancel. The last hymn had been sung, and the congregation were waiting for the bishop to pronounce the benediction, when suddenly there was a commotion at the west door of the nave. The silence was broken by a woman's shrill voice. I could see her now, probably in her thirties and rather dishevelled.

She began walking unsteadily up the centre aisle, shouting as she came. She was evidently intoxicated. Yet nobody tried to restrain her. She reached the chancel step. Her arms were stretched out in an eloquent appeal, and there was a look of anguish on her face. She was almost level with me now, and I feared that she was going to accost me, perhaps to disagree with something I had said in my sermon. But no, she walked past me, continuing to call out.

**Top: Lyse fjord and Kjerag, near Stavanger, Norway**

**Below: Reindeer.**

Still nobody moved. For, although she was evidently under the influence of alcohol, what she was saying was apparently perfectly rational. 'What is she saying?' I asked the Dean. He whispered a translation to me. She was a sinner, she was saying, a prostitute with an illegitimate child, and a drug addict: was there grace for *her*? The bishop had welcomed everybody at the beginning of the service: but would there be a welcome for *her*?

The woman had nearly reached the high altar now, where the bishop was standing and waiting. He did not move. There was no look of disapproval on his face; only a gentle smile of compassion. She flung herself sobbing into his arms. He did not reject her. He held her and hugged her, and spoke to her of the Saviour's forgiving love.

I could not help thinking of the Pharisees' taunt about Jesus: 'This man welcomes sinners' (Luke 15:2).

FOOTNOTES

1. Gwyn Jones, *A History of the Vikings* (OUP, revised edition, 1984), p. 196.

2. *Ibid.*, p. 2

3. See the article 'Stottiana for 1000 years' in *The Genealogical Quarterly*, Vol. xix No.1, 1952.

4. K. S. Latourette, *The History of the Expansion of Christianity* (Eyre and Spottiswoode, 1938), Vol. II, p. 123.

5. From an obituary in *The Messenger*, news from Stavanger International Church.

# Some Icelandic Birds

*'God created . . . every winged bird according to its kind.'*
*(Genesis 1:21)*

*Overall*: Barrow's Goldeneye, sometimes called 'the Iceland Duck'. *Bottom left to right*: Black-tailed Godwit; Arctic Tern; Fulmar, revealing its characteristic 'tube nose'.

# 3. Richard Wurmbrand

## *Persecuted in Romania*

I**T WAS A FRIDAY IN OCTOBER 1966 IN LONDON.** The speaker stood before us – tall, grey, gaunt and haggard. He still bore the marks of torture. At one point during his address he had lifted his shirt to expose deep scars in his torso. Yet his spirit was free of bitterness. He exuded only gentleness and love, in stark contrast to the brutality he had experienced. When he had finished, there was no applause. We had been shocked into silence. There was nothing to say.

The speaker was Richard Wurmbrand, who had just been released after fourteen years of imprisonment and torture in Romania. During the following years he would tell his story in his books *Tortured for Christ* (1967) and *In God's Underground* (1968).

Richard Wurmbrand was born of atheistic Jewish parents in 1909 in Bucharest. He was orphaned while still a child and later plunged recklessly into the life of a playboy. But in 1936 he was converted through the testimony of a village carpenter, who gave him a Bible. Soon afterwards, impressed by her husband's changed behaviour, his wife Sabina also believed,

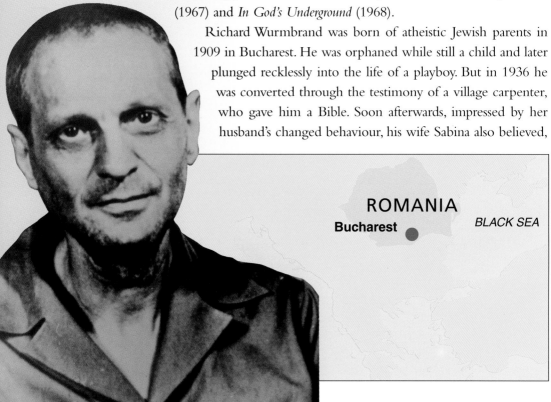

**ROMANIA**
**Bucharest** ●     *BLACK SEA*

**This polluted Romanian townscape typifies the period of Communist rule.**

and both of them were baptized. He was then ordained into the Norwegian Lutheran Church, and served in their mission in Bucharest. During the years of German occupation he was three times arrested for evangelizing Russian prisoners-of-war. The Nazis gave him his first bitter taste of prison, interrogation and torture.

In 1944 the Soviet Communists seized Romania. Then, while many official church leaders compromised and collaborated with them, Richard Wurmbrand began a ministry to the faithful underground church, witnessing both to Russian soldiers and to the enslaved Romanian people, teaching the Word of God and smuggling in Bibles and Christian literature.

It was risky work, and in February 1948 the secret police kidnapped him in the street. His fourteen-year ordeal of imprisonment (in two stages) began. The prison authorities subjected him to every torture which human cruelty could devise, hoping to break his spirit and induce him to betray his friends. This is what he wrote of that time:

> *I had been brutally beaten and kicked, derided, starved, pressured, questioned* ad nauseam, *threatened and neglected.*[1]

But he refused to give in or to renounce his faith. He even continued his underground evangelism by developing a morse code and tapping messages to fellow-prisoners in neighbouring cells.

The worst trial he had to endure was three years in solitary confinement in a dank underground cell, cut off from all communication with people except for his prison guards and his interrogators. For a human being as sensitive as Richard Wurmbrand, this was a ghastly experience:

*I spent three years alone in a cell thirty feet below ground, never seeing sun, moon or stars, flowers or snow . . .*[2]

He had no Bible or other book or any personal possession. Alone with his thoughts, and in order to preserve his sanity, he developed his own special routine. Sleeping by day and keeping awake all night, he told himself jokes and invented new ones. He played chess with himself, using pieces made from bread. He made friends with a spider, which later froze to death. He composed 300 poems and committed them to memory. Above all, he prepared and preached a new sermon to himself every night, as if he were preaching in church. Each began 'Dear brothers and sisters', and each ended with a decisive 'Amen'. He turned the essence of each sermon into rhyme in order to help him remember them, and after his release he wrote down 350 of them, twenty-two of which were published in his book *Sermons in Solitary Confinement* (1969).

The thoughts which flowed into his sermons were mostly intimate conversations with God, with angels, and with human beings like his wife and their son Mihai. They were introspective and imaginative, mostly lucid but sometimes bordering on the insane, as if his mind had become unhinged. All his human emotions – love, pain, anger, compassion, hope, doubt and despair – were expressed. They kept him sane. 'Alone in my cell,' he wrote, 'cold, hungry and in rags, I danced for joy every night.'

**Richard and Sabina Wurmbrand.**

In June 1964, under a general amnesty resulting from an East–West thaw, all political prisoners were released, and Richard Wurmbrand was set free. When he reached home, he said to his wife: 'Don't think I've simply come from misery to happiness! I've come from the joy of being with Christ in prison to the joy of being with him in my family.'[4]

Richard Wurmbrand was ransomed by some Norwegian Christians, who paid $10,000 to the Romanian government for his release. He was reluctant to leave his country and his ministry, but the underground church leaders urged him to go to the West, in

**A canoe on the swollen waters of the river Danube, Romania.**

order to be a voice for the persecuted church throughout the world. When he left, the Romanian authorities warned him not to speak against the Communist regime, threatening him with kidnapping, assassination or slander about an invented scandal. But Wurmbrand ignored these threats. In 1966, as related above, he came to London. He also testified before the Internal Security Committee of the U.S. Senate.

In subsequent years Richard and Sabina founded the Christian Mission to the Communist World, now known as Release International, and similar missions in almost 30 countries. He faithfully toured the world, seeking to make known how widespread is the persecution of Christians. In 1990, following the fall of Ceausescu, they returned to Romania after an exile of twenty-five years, and received a hero's welcome. Richard died in February 2001, aged 91.

My first visit to Romania took place in May 1987, while Nicolae Ceausescu was still Head of State and leading a repressive Communist regime. My travelling companion was Alex Williams, who is familiar with much of Eastern Europe. We entered the country as tourists and spent two days bird watching in the Danube Delta, which consists of about 2,000 square miles of watery wilderness and supports a breeding colony of about 2,500 pairs of White Pelicans.

The established Church in Romania is of course the Orthodox Church. The Roman Catholic Church is smaller, and there is the usual

**The Second Baptist Church, Oradea today and (inset) under Ceausescu.**

**Josef Tson, former pastor of the Second Baptist Church, Oradea, Romania.**

spectrum of Protestant churches. But it was the Baptists who had sent me several indirect messages (through couriers), inviting me to visit them. They had suffered much from Communist repression. In 1958 six hundred Baptist pastors had been dismissed, and either were imprisoned or disappeared. The 200 pastors left were mostly elderly, theologically liberal or suspected of being informers. At the time of my visit, therefore, although there were about 1000 Baptist churches, there were only 160 pastors, leaving 840 churches with lay leadership.

In 1974 Josef Tson, who had graduated at Oxford and had himself for some years been pastor of the Second Baptist Church in Oradea, had had the courage to stage a confrontation with the authorities on religious freedom. He wrote a 'Christian Manifesto' which, having been smuggled out to the West, was put into President Ceausescu's hands in Washington DC by President Richard Nixon. Some easing of tension followed. But in 1981 Josef was sent for by the secret police and given the alternative of prison or exile. After consultation with his church leaders, they unanimously decided on exile. So he developed a ministry in the United States, founding the Romanian Missionary Society, pastoring expatriate Romanians, and translating Christian books into Romanian.

The following year the Second Baptist Church of Oradea called two dynamic lay leaders to serve as their pastors. Both are doctors. Dr Nic Gheorghita, an endocrinologist, is the older man and a delightfully encouraging father-figure. The other is Dr Paul Negrut, a clinical psychologist, in his thirties and a born leader. But during the five years before my visit the authorities had been playing a cat-and-mouse game with these men over their appointment and over the building of a new church. First, they were threatened with the demolition of their old church, and a government bulldozer was parked ominously outside. Then they got permission to purchase a property and obtained written approval of their building plans, only to have these revoked when a new Minister of Religious Affairs was appointed.

**A Romanian woman in peasant clothing.**

**A Romanian farmhouse on the banks of the Danube.**

Arriving at church on a Sunday, I was expecting a small congregation, since I knew that Sunday was a working day. But the place was packed with 2,500 in the morning and 3,000 in the evening. The men were sitting on one side and the women on the other. The side and centre aisles were blocked with people standing three or four abreast, and the congregation spilled out into the courtyard. The gallery was occupied by a choir 250 strong. The singing, led by a conductor, an electronic organ and a synthesizer, was very polished, and the tunes were mostly traditional Romanian melodies, which seemed an appropriate combination of strength and melancholy. Nearly all the women wore colourful head-scarves. All ages were represented, and there were

**Dr Paul Negrut (*right*) a clinical psychologist and joint leader of the Second Baptist Church, Oradea with Dr Nic Gheorghita (*left*) an endocrinologist.**

as many men as women. The services lasted two hours, and at each about six people gave their testimonies in preparation for their baptism the following Sunday. The whole service was most inspiring, expressing Christian assurance, reverence, courage and joy.

Yet all the time one could not forget the background of state repression. There would be at least ten informers in the congregation, we were told. And during lunch in Paul Negrut's garden he kept his radio on throughout our conversation, in order to block (or at least interfere with) the bugging devices he felt sure were operating. He told me horrific stories of being interrogated by the secret police, of an attempt to electrocute him and his family by connecting high tension overhead wires to the gutter and drainpipe of his house, and of threatening innuendos about the number of car accidents which took place in Oradea each week.

So I asked Paul if I would have his goodwill to draft a letter to President Ceausescu, to be signed by some British leaders of parliament and church, pointing out that Oradea's Second Baptist Church is the largest Baptist Church in Europe, and a credit to the country, and urging both the building of the new church and the ending of the harassment of its leaders. Paul readily agreed, on the ground that the state was very sensitive to Western opinion. And indeed a telegram and letter to President Ceausescu some years previously, sent by FEET (the

Fellowship of European Evangelical Theologians), asking for the return to Josef Tson of his confiscated library, were successful. His library was returned to him at once. So several letters were sent to the President, encouraged by the British Ambassador. Although no reply was ever received, who knows whether they were helpful?

Certainly the harassment seems to have eased a little. But in any case the church leaders refused to be intimidated. The large attendances at Sunday services, the 150-200 baptisms a year, the Monday night Bible studies for about 500 young people, 'The School of the Prophets' which was training lay leaders, and the fact that when Josef Tson spoke every Sunday afternoon on the Radio Free Europe programme, it is said that 80 per cent of the population listened to him – all this is evidence that materialism (whether Communist or Capitalist) can never satisfy the human spirit.

Since the overthrow and execution of President Ceausescu in 1989 I have been privileged to return to Oradea twice. The new Emmanuel Baptist Church has been built, seating 4,000. The Emmanuel Bible Institute has become the Emmanuel University of Oradea. Several social projects have been developed, including an orphanage for HIV-infected children. The 1990 'Torch of Freedom' award was presented to Paul Negrut by the British Prime Minister. And a steady stream of gifted young people are entering the pastorate and other ministries. Truly Christ is building his church, as he said he would, 'and the gates of Hades will not overcome it' (Matt. 16:18).

FOOTNOTES

1. *Tortured for Christ* (Hodder and Stoughton, 1967), p. 38.

2. Richard Wurmbrand, *Sermons in Solitary Confinement* (Hodder and Stoughton, 1969), p. 7. Re-released as *With God in Solitary Confinement* (Living Sacrifice).

3. *In God's Underground* (Hodder and Stoughton, 1969), p. 54.

4. *In God's Underground*, p. 178.

# 4. The Apostle Paul
## A missionary journey in Turkey

**Black Sea**

**TURKEY**

THE TOWERING FIGURE OF THE EARLY CHURCH was the apostle Paul. So much so that he has sometimes been called 'the *real* founder of Christianity'. By this critics have meant that Paul corrupted the simple, unsophisticated religion of Jesus into the complicated theologizing which we tend to associate with him. This theory does not fit the facts, however, as Dr David Wenham has demonstrated.[1] Nevertheless, Paul did have a unique role as 'the apostle to the Gentiles', since Christ called him specifically to open the door of faith to the non-Jewish world.[2]

**Detail from 'St Paul the Apostle' by Martino de Bartolommeo (1369–1434).**

It was in April 1978 that my friends Dick and Thea van Halsema[3] and I went together in the footsteps of St Paul, following the route of his first missionary journey, as recorded by Luke in Acts 13 and 14. It is highly appropriate that Syrian Antioch should have been the launching pad for the international Christian mission, since its population was extremely cosmopolitan, and it was in Antioch that the followers of Jesus were first nicknamed 'Christians' (Acts 11:26). The city was both beautiful and wealthy. It boasted theatres, temples, swimming pools, a race course and a large market. Soon after Paul's stay there it became known as the third largest city in the empire, after Rome and Alexandria.

Twelve miles south-west of Antioch, at the mouth of the River Orontes, was the port of Seleucia, although all that remains of the Roman harbour today is some massive squared stones jutting out into the sea in two arms. 'They were engineers, those Romans', muttered George our guide, overcome with admiration.

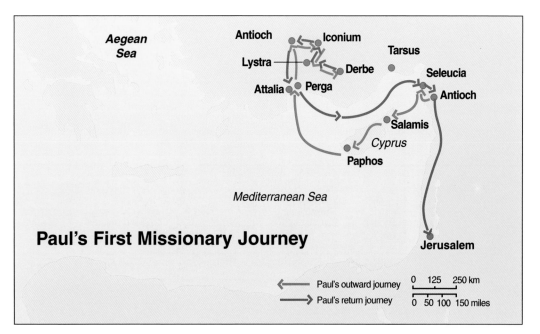

**Paul's First Missionary Journey**

Aegean Sea

Antioch
Iconium
Tarsus
Lystra
Derbe
Seleucia
Attalia
Perga
Antioch
Salamis
Cyprus
Paphos

Mediterranean Sea

Jerusalem

Paul's outward journey
Paul's return journey

0   125   250 km
0  50 100 150 miles

**Dick van Halsema examines the huge stone blocks remaining from the Roman harbour at Seleucia, port for Syrian Antioch.**

Paul and Barnabas, accompanied by Barnabas' young nephew or cousin, John Mark, set sail from Seleucia to Cyprus (Barnabas' home) and from there to Perga in Pamphylia, on what today is called the 'turquoise coast' of the Mediterranean. We omitted Cyprus from our itinerary and instead reached Perga overland. Its ruins, partly excavated and restored, give one a clear impression of the glories it once possessed. But Paul and Barnabas did not linger on the coast. Instead, they pushed on north over the Taurus mountains to the Galatian plateau beyond, in particular to Pisidian Antioch. This was a distance of nearly 150 miles. If the missionaries walked it, it would have taken them at least eight days. So perhaps they travelled on horseback.

Before they set out, however, they suffered a setback. John Mark, their assistant, left them and returned to Jerusalem (though later he was reconciled). All sorts of theories have been advanced to explain what happened. Certainly Paul regarded Mark's departure as a defection (Acts 15:37, 38). Certainly too the apostle was sick with a debilitating illness. 'It was because of an illness that I first preached the gospel to you', he wrote later to the Galatians (4:13). Moreover it seems to have disfigured him in some way, so that the Galatians might have treated him with contempt (4:14). It had also affected his eyesight, so that if possible they would have torn out their own eyes and given them to him (4:15; *cf.* 6:11).

Sir William Ramsay suggested years ago that Paul suffered from 'a

33

**Tiered seating of the theatre, Perga.**

**Part of the ruins of the Roman city of Perga, Asia Minor.**

**The author in an Arab *keffiyeh* in Turkey.**

species of chronic malaria fever', which the ancient Greeks and Romans knew and feared; that it involved 'very distressing and prostrating paroxysms', together with stabbing headaches 'like a red-hot bar thrust through the forehead' (perhaps what Paul later called his 'thorn in the flesh' – 2 Cor. 12:7); and that it was his fever which made it necessary for him to leave the enervating climate of the coastal plain, in spite of the rigorous climb involved, in order to seek the bracing cool of the Galatian plateau some 3,500 feet above sea level.[4]

At all events, they were in a hurry and did not stop to evangelize Perga. Was Mark already homesick, missing his mother, her spacious Jerusalem home and the servants? Did he resent the fact that Paul seemed to be eclipsing his uncle Barnabas? Did he disagree with Paul's bold policy of Gentile evangelism? Or did Mark simply not relish the stiff climb over the Taurus mountains, which were known to be infested with brigands? I have often wondered if he did not like the look of the mosquitoes in the swamps of Pamphylia, even if at that time the link between mosquitoes and malaria was not understood.

What will have taken Paul and Barnabas a hard slog of several days, we were able to accomplish in only a few hours' drive. Pisidian Antioch had been a Greek colony before the Emperor Augustus made it a Roman garrison town. But now nothing survives except a few arches of a first century BC Roman aqueduct, in a crevice of which a pair of Black Redstarts had built their nest.

There must have been a sizeable Jewish population too, for Paul and Barnabas went to the synagogue on the Sabbath day, and Luke gives us a full account of Paul's sermon. Beginning with an Old Testament survey, he proclaimed the good news of forgiveness to those who trust in the crucified and resurrected Jesus.

The second Galatian city to which Paul and Barnabas brought the gospel was Iconium, situated nearly 100 miles south-east of Pisidian Antioch, and overlooking the broad plateau which lies between the Taurus and the Sultan mountain ranges. Today it is Turkey's fourth largest city of Konya, a centre of agriculture and commerce. It was another long trek for the missionaries, although they must have been refreshed by the

**A Turkish shepherd near the remains of the Roman city of Pisidian Antioch.**

**White Stork's nest at Konya, ancient Iconium.**

beauties of plain, river, lake and mountain all round them. For when they reached Lystra, Paul spoke of 'the living God who made the heavens and the earth and the sea and all that is in them' (Acts 14:15).

Lystra, the third city visited, no longer figures on any Turkish map, but its site is believed to be just west of the village of Hatunsaray. Nothing has been excavated, however. All that was visible was a large, grass-covered, rather oblong tumulus, occupied by moles, ground squirrels and a fox. Scattered about were lichen-covered stones, pedestals and broken pieces of columns, inhabited by shy Black-eared Wheatears and a pair of Hoopoes.

Paul was stoned by an angry mob in Lystra, dragged out of the city and left for dead. But such was his resilience that he had recovered sufficiently to leave the following morning for Derbe, the fourth and last Galatian town he was to visit on his first missionary journey.

It was a trudge south-east to Derbe of at least sixty miles. How could Paul's bruised and battered body manage it? 'I bear on my body the marks of Jesus', he was soon to write to the Galatians (6:17). Of course the companionship of Barnabas will have encouraged him. But I could not help wondering if his spirit had also been cheered by the spectacular, snow-capped mountains around him, by the White Storks nesting on the village rooftops, and by the pretty song of the Calandra Larks. Luke gives us no information about his mission in Derbe, only that 'they preached the good news in that city and won a large number of disciples' (Acts 14:21).

We, however, had some difficulty in finding the Derbe site. It is

*Above*: **Kapi Camii, one of the many fine mosques in Konya, ancient Iconium.**

*Below*: **The Taurus Montains, through which Paul travelled on his second missionary journey.**

known locally as Kerti Höyuk, meaning a 'mound' or 'tumulus'. Mustafa, a local farmer, guided us out into the open countryside and then came to an abrupt halt. 'It's an hour's walk from here,' he said, adding rather menacingly 'and another hour back!'

Undeterred by his implied dissuader, we set out on foot at a brisk pace. It was already early evening, and the sun was setting behind the frowning face of Karadag ('the Black Mountain'). We made good progress, and now the great green tumulus of Kerti Höyuk, which had once been Derbe, was only a few hundred yards ahead of us. Here Mustafa declared with decision that we could go no further, for the mound was surrounded by an impassable swamp. From it, however, a dozen pairs of Ruddy Shelduck took to the air, their cinnamon-coloured bodies gleaming in the evening light, and honking in a rather melancholy fashion. In future I shall always associate Lystra with Hoopoes and Derbe with Ruddy Shelduck.

Paul's itinerary after Derbe was to retrace his steps to Lystra, Iconium and Pisidian Antioch, strengthening the newly planted churches, and then to sail home. By contrast, we drove to Syria. Our route took us through the so-called 'Cilician Gates', the picturesque name given to the narrowest gorge through the East Taurus mountains – a pass used over the centuries by armies marching in both directions. Here roam

**Remains of the ancient Roman 'Cleopatra's Gate,' Tarsus.**

**An old quarter of Tarsus, near 'St Paul's Well'.**

black goats, for whose wool Cilicia was famous. It was woven into cloth called 'cilicium' and may well explain Paul's trade of 'tent-making'.

A few miles on, at the foot of the Taurus range, lies Tarsus, where Paul was born and brought up. He described it as 'no mean city' (Acts 21:39), but it is rather undistinguished today.

After visiting an ancient Roman stone well known as 'St Paul's well', we were shown round the local museum. All the exhibits were Greek, Roman and Muslim. I drew the young curator's attention to the strange fact that his museum contained no single reference to the man who must surely be the most famous son of Tarsus, the Christian apostle Paul. The curator nodded his acknowledgement of the fact. Supposing, I went on, I were to present the museum with a professionally crafted exhibit featuring Paul's life and work, would he accept and display it? Yes, he would, he said, but added immediately that he would have to refer the matter to the authorities in Ankara.

So on my return to London, I composed a letter to the appropriate authorities in Tarsus and Ankara and had it translated into Turkish. In it I marshalled all the arguments I could think of for having such a display in the Tarsus museum, especially the attraction it would be to American and European tourists. It would not be a piece of Christian propaganda

**A misty morning near the mouth of the River Orontes.**

or be offensive to Muslims, I added, but a straightforward, factual account of Paul's remarkable career. In the light of these things, I concluded, would the authorities in Ankara accept such a gift and authorize its display?

That was 5th May 1978. Nearly a quarter of a century later, I am still awaiting a response.

FOOTNOTES

1. See David Wenham, *Paul: Follower of Jesus or Founder of Christianity?* (IVP, 1995).

2. *e.g.* Acts 14:27; Rom. 1:5, 15:15, 16; Gal. 1:16; 2:8; Eph. 3:8, etc.

3. The Rev. Dr Richard van Halsema was President of the Reformed Bible College in Grand Rapids, Michigan from 1966 to 1987. He, his wife Thea and their five children did a mini-bus tour through Asia Minor in 1962, which Thea wrote up in her charming book entitled *Safari for Seven* (Baker, 1967). They have also led several tour groups to Greece and Turkey.

4. William M. Ramsay, *St Paul the Traveller and the Roman Citizen* (Hodder and Stoughton, 1895, 11th ed. undated), pp. 92-97.

# 5. Temple Gairdner
## *Scholar in Cairo, Egypt*

IT IS A HUMBLING EXPERIENCE FOR ANY EUROPEAN OR AMERICAN to visit Egypt, and become aware of the brilliance of its ancient civilization. The pyramid age reached its zenith in the middle of the third millennium BC, and the three 'great' pyramids (royal tombs), situated at Giza, a few miles south-west of Cairo, were included among the seven wonders of the world. The largest is claimed as the greatest building ever erected by human genius. Its geometric precision is phenomenal. It is constructed of more than two million blocks of limestone and granite, each weighing an average of two and a half tons. At the time of the Exodus, when the reigning Pharaoh was probably Rameses II during the first half of the thirteenth century BC, the pyramids had already been there for a thousand years.

**Temple Gairdner of Cairo as a young man.**

Although it is a Muslim country, Egypt also has a longstanding Christian tradition. The Coptic Orthodox Church claims that it was founded by Mark the evangelist, who preached and was probably martyred in Alexandria, which then became one of the great centres of Christian culture and influence in the early church, alongside Jerusalem and Rome. In the third century AD Clement and Origen, leading Greek church fathers, taught, wrote and debated in Alexandria. And in the fourth century Athanasius of Alexandria, almost single-handed, rescued the church from the heresy of Arius, who taught that Jesus was not God, but only a very superior created being.

When I visited Cairo in 1973, the Coptic Orthodox Church was experiencing a remarkable movement of biblical renewal. Patriarch Shenuda III (known in Egypt as 'the Pope') was preaching every Friday night in the huge Orthodox Cathedral to between five and ten thousand people, answering

their questions and endeavouring to relate the ancient Orthodox faith to the contemporary world. A similar meeting was held every Sunday night in Alexandria.

One of the most striking figures of the Coptic Orthodox Church at that time was Abuna ('Father') Zakaria Botros. He was an Orthodox priest who in 1964 had an evangelical experience of Christ, which changed the direction of his ministry. He was now expounding Scripture and answering questions to 1000 or more people, using relay and closed circuit television, every Tuesday and Thursday evening in the hall of his church, St Mark's. Some friends and I attended a part of his meeting one Thursday evening. He was faithfully expounding Galatians 5 and 6. Following his address, he asked a minister of the Coptic Evangelical church (the indigenous Presbyterian church) to close in prayer.

**One of the great pyramids outside Cairo.**

**Father Zakaria Botros, Orthodox Egyptian priest.**

Then we were granted a private interview with Father Zakaria. Dressed in the black robes of an Orthodox priest, he was carrying a silver cross in one hand and a fat, black, well-thumbed Bible in the other. A winsome smile peeped through his bushy black beard. He spoke of his ministry, and told us that he relied in his Bible study (1) on the Holy Spirit, (2) on the ancient Orthodox fathers, and (3) on Matthew Henry (an eighteenth century English non-conformist expositor) – in that order! He also told us that he had baptized 100 Muslims in St Mark's and added with a shining face 'I hope to see Egypt for Christ'.

Unfortunately, not long afterwards, this faithful gospel preacher was silenced. An Orthodox theologian wrote a series of articles contradicting the gospel of justification by grace alone through faith alone, and the church authorities withdrew his license to teach.

In December 2001, having heard that Father Zakaria was now in England, ministering in a Coptic Orthodox Church on the south coast, I went to see him. Now sixty-eight years old, his beard had turned grey and he was wearing spectacles, but the same robes, the same smile and the same fire made it easy to recognize him.

He told me more about his conversion. It was Cyril of Jerusalem, the fourth century Greek Church father, who had helped him to understand the way of salvation, how Christ had accomplished in one hour on the cross what we cannot do by years of good deeds.

**Domes and minarets of the great mosque, Cairo.**

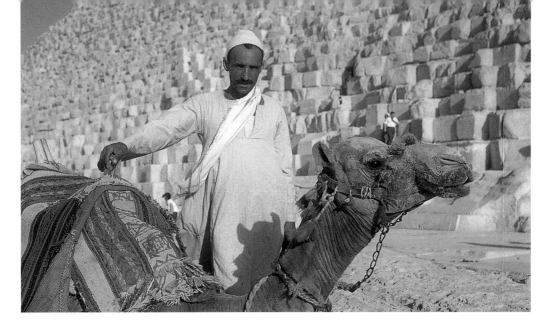

As he proclaimed this gospel of God's sheer grace, opposition soon
arose, first from the church and then from the state. Accused by the
hierarchy of teaching Protestant doctrines, he was exiled to a little
church in the Nile Delta, and later forbidden to preach for a year. From
1969-78, however, he taught large crowds at St Mark's Church in Cairo,
which is where I met him in 1973. He proclaimed boldly the good
news that if we open our hearts to the Saviour, we will be saved.
Forbidden a second time to preach, now for nine years, 'it was a marvellous time', he said, because he had the opportunity to study and to
develop his programme of lay education.

But because Father Zakaria also evangelized Muslims, and by 1988
had baptized 500, he began to be hunted by the secret police. He was
twice imprisoned in Egypt, exiled to Australia for three years, blacklist-
ed and now serving in the UK. But he has an Arabic web-site which is
visited by people from all over the world. He has also published his training booklet. He showed me a copy. It develops six stages of discipleship,
which are all about Christ – receiving him, knowing him, standing firm
in him, becoming like him, and witnessing to him. Prominent at the
beginning of the booklet is the text which means much to him, as it does
to me: 'Behold, I stand at the door, and knock: if any man hear my voice,
and open the door, I will come in to him, and will sup with him, and he
with me' (Revelation 3:20, KJV). Father Zakaria continues:

> How many times did the Lord Jesus knock on your heart? How many
> times were his knocks both sweet and light, coming in the form of
> earthly blessings, health and success? Have you recognised these light

43

**A street scene in modern Cairo.**

*knocks, or has he been constrained by you to use heavy and fearful knocks, which come in the form of tribulations, illnesses, problems and hardships that you have faced? . . . The Lord takes every opportunity to knock on the door of our hearts.*[1]

Before leaving Cairo in 1973 I visited its three Christian cemeteries, where some of the evangelical heroes of the recent past are buried.

First, in the war cemetery is the tomb of Oswald Chambers. Having served as an itinerant preacher-evangelist, and as Principal of the Bible Training College in Clapham Common, south London, Oswald Chambers announced his intention 'to go out to Egypt to help the men in the Forces'. As Superintendent of the Egyptian YMCA, he ministered to the soldiers in the desert camps from 1915 to 1917, but suddenly fell ill with appendicitis and died. He is best remembered for his prolific writing ministry – thirty books, lovingly compiled by his wife from her shorthand notes of his addresses, translated into about sixty-five languages, and specially his anthology of daily readings *My Utmost for His Highest*. He was also a remarkable man. A colleague described him as not one man but many – 'artist, poet, philosopher, preacher and teacher, comedian'.[2] Yet, despite these manifold distinctions, what is inscribed on his tombstone is simply 'Oswald Chambers – a believer in Jesus Christ'.

More elaborate is the grave of 'Borden of Yale' in the American cemetery of Old Cairo. William Borden was born in 1887 into a wealthy Chicago family, was converted at Moody Memorial Church as a teenager, and went up to Yale in 1909. There Samuel Zwemer persuaded him to become a missionary to Muslims in China. Three years later he sailed for Cairo to study Arabic, en route for China, having

**The sphinx, a huge mythological stone figure, near the pyramids.**

**British military tombstone of Oswald Chambers in Egypt.**

renounced his inheritance of nearly one million dollars. But soon after his arrival in Cairo he contracted spinal meningitis and died. Under his pillow some friends found a scribbled note: 'No Reserve! No Retreat! No Regrets!' He was only twenty-five.[3]

Thirdly, in the cemetery belonging to the Church Missionary Society, are the graves of Temple Gairdner and his close friend and fellow-worker, Douglas Thornton.

Temple Gairdner was born in Scotland in 1873, and came to both personal faith in Christ and missionary commitment while he was an undergraduate at Trinity College, Oxford. He became an active member of the Oxford Inter-Collegiate Christian Union (OICCU) and was its president in 1895. Two years previously at the Keswick Convention he had signed the pledge taken by members of the Student Volunteer Missionary Union: 'It is my purpose, if God permit, to become a foreign missionary'.

The Church Missionary Society accepted him in 1897, and in 1899 he was ordained deacon in St Paul's Cathedral. All this time his mind had been focussing on the Muslim world of the Middle East, and specially on Cairo which he described as '*the* centre of Islam, *par excellence*'.[4] Already, even before he arrived in Cairo, lifetime goals were beginning to formulate in his mind: to master Arabic, to create a body of Arab Christian literature for educated Muslims, and to penetrate to the heart of Islam.

It is difficult to paint in words an adequate picture of Temple Gairdner's colourful personality. He had a powerful intellect, so that

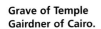

**Grave of Temple Gairdner of Cairo.**

**Elaborate minarets in Cairo.**

people spoke of him either as an absent-minded scholar or as a genius. He was a brilliant linguist. He was also very artistic, appreciating all things beautiful, and he could not live without music. He became a devoted husband and father. He had a great capacity for friendship, and he lived simply. Everything he did he undertook with enthusiasm and prayer, often enlivened by an almost boyish sense of humour. And one of the highest honours paid to him was his teacher's saying that 'he was more Egyptian than the Egyptians'.[5]

Thus Temple Gairdner was an authentic, cross-cultural messenger of the gospel, who identified with those to whom he had been sent. Here are some examples:

**1. Language.** He mastered Arabic, as he had determined, so that he wrote both a grammar of *Egyptian Colloquial Arabic* (1917) and *The Phonetics of Arabic* (1925), which quickly became standard works.

**2. Dialogue.** Long before the concept of inter-faith 'dialogue' had become fashionable, Gairdner was pioneering the way, convening a study group and engaging in public debate with scholarly Muslim teachers. 'I cannot say what a pleasure it is', he wrote, 'to feel oneself really one with this people as we sit side by side in free, vivacious, amicable yet regulated exchange of thought.'[6]

**3. Literature.** Temple Gairdner envisaged 'a great literary campaign for Christ',[7] in which he and Douglas Thornton did the writing, editing, printing, publishing and distributing of tracts, whose topics would be some of the major centuries-long issues between Christianity and Islam.

In addition, they produced a magazine entitled *Orient and Occident* (popularly known as 'O and O'), whose circulation steadily climbed to 3000. In all their writing, although they acknowledged the necessity of apologetics (as in the Gospels and Epistles), they also resolved to humanize the tone and temper in which the debate was conducted. 'We need, in our message to the Muslims', he wrote, 'not the dry cracked note of disputation, but the song note of joyous witness, tender invitation.'[8] He was always fair, thoughtful, humble and courteous.

**4. Poetry.** In addition to the tracts and the magazine, Temple Gairdner even wrote and published poetry in Arabic. According to his biographer, he was probably the only westerner of whom the *Muktataf* (the leading Arabic literary review of Cairo) wrote that he 'must be accounted an Arabic poet of genius'.[9]

**5. Music.** Temple Gairdner was a musician to his fingertips. So he

**Part of a music manuscript for *Joseph* by Temple Gairdner.**

not only composed hymns, but set them to the Near Eastern tunes he had collected. Today he would be called an 'ethnomusicologist'.

**6. Drama.** Gairdner was determined that Egypt should *see* the gospel. So he wrote a number of plays on biblical themes, like *Joseph and his brothers*, an Old Testament passion play (1921), *Saul and Stephen* (1922), *The Good Samaritan*, a New Testament morality play (1923) and *King Hezekiah*, a tragical drama (1925).

Temple Gairdner has been described by Bishop Kenneth Cragg, himself a leading Islam specialist, as 'a seminal figure in Christian-Muslim relations'.[10] For twenty-nine years he devoted his heart and mind, time and energy to 'incarnational' mission, seeking to penetrate the Muslim's world with the good news of Jesus Christ.

FOOTNOTES

1. Father Zakaria Botros, *How do I start with Christ?* (1992), pp. 24, 25.
2. D. W. Lambert, *Oswald Chambers, an unbribed soul* (Marshall Morgan and Scott, 1968), p. 21. See also *Oswald Chambers, his life and work* by his widow Bertha (Marshall Morgan and Scott, 1959) and his life story in *Abandoned to God* by David McCasland (Discovery House Publishers, 1993)
3. See Mrs Howard Taylor, *Borden of Yale* (1926; revised edition 1952).
4. Constance E. Padwick, *Temple Gairdner of Cairo* (SPCK, 1929), p. 72.
5. *Ibid.,* p. 83.
6. *Ibid.,* p. 84.
7. *Ibid.,* p. 149.
8. *Ibid.,* p. 158.
9. *Ibid.,* p. 313.
10. See Bishop Kenneth Cragg's entry 'W. H. T. Gairdner' in *Biographical Dictionary of Christian Missions*, ed. Gerald H. Anderson (Eerdmans, 1998).

# 6. Festo Kivengere

## *African evangelist*

I CHOOSE AS REPRESENTATIVE OF AFRICA THE MAN who has been
acclaimed the best-known and best-loved twentieth-century
African evangelist, Festo Kivengere, who died in 1988.

He was born into a remote, semi-nomadic tribe, the Bahima of
south-western Uganda, and used to herd cattle as a boy. In fact he is a
fine example of the 'local boy made good' syndrome, in that he was a
pupil in Kigezi High School, later became a teacher there, and then,
after serving as Schools Supervisor in the Kigezi district, was elected in
1972 the first African bishop of Kigezi. At the same time he became a
world figure, conducting missions in many countries, especially in the
UK, the US and Australia.

Festo was a product of the East African revival, which began in the
1930s and brought spiritual renewal to many individuals and churches.
The revival brethren (the '*balokole*' or 'saved ones') acknowledged him as

MEDITERRANEAN SEA

RED SEA

**AFRICA**

Lake Turkana

Lake Albert **Uganda**

Lake Victoria **Indian Ocean**

**Festo Kivengere preaching in London.**

one of their leaders, for he shared their concerns and used their vocabulary, speaking of the need for 'brokenness' before God, and for 'walking in the light' before him and his people. Nevertheless, he had an independent mind and challenged the *balokole's* tendency to Pharisaism, reducing the Christian life to inflexible rules and regulations. Festo was fundamentally Christ-centred in his faith and life. '*Real* revival', he would say, 'is Jesus Christ himself'.[1]

Festo Kivengere was a very gifted speaker. Inheriting from his tribal and pastoral background a love for story-telling, he could captivate his audience with vivid pictures. He was relaxed and confident, and though he felt deeply what he was talking about, he would enliven his messages with delightful touches of African humour. Being a voracious reader, and having a natural eloquence, he was able to extemporize with great freedom. He was also extremely bold in his applications, challenging his listeners to respond to the Word of God.

Like all Christian leaders Festo struggled with the temptation to pride and vainglory. He and I sometimes spoke about it together, since we shared in a number of missions and conferences. In July 1972 we were both speakers at the Keswick Convention in the north of England. I reminded him of one of his own sayings, which I had heard him use, and which seemed to me to expose the ludicrous nature of pride. 'You've only got to take the throne of your personality and sit yourself on it, and you see at once that you are conspicuously too small for it.'[2]

The author with
Corey Widmer at the
equator in Uganda.

Bishop James
Hannington,
martyred in the
nineteenth century
in Uganda.

Some three months after Keswick, Festo Kivengere was consecrated bishop in St Paul's Cathedral, Namirembe, Kampala, and enthroned as Bishop of Kigezi in St Peter's Cathedral, Kabale. He felt uncomfortable with the language of 'enthronement', the accompanying ceremonial and the colourful episcopal vesture (purple cassock and scarlet chimere). In anticipation of possible criticism he reminded some friends of the late Yohana Omari, who had been Bishop of Morogoro and the first African bishop in Tanzania. Bishop Yohana had recalled the Gospels' story of the colt on which Jesus rode into Jerusalem. Before he mounted the colt, the people threw their beautiful garments on it. Just so, he added, 'under the scarlet robes of an Anglican bishop will lie a donkey for the Master to ride on . . .'. Bishop Festo quoted this in the course of his enthronement address, and added: 'I want to be like the little donkey our Lord chose to ride on to enter Jerusalem. They laid their robes on it and shouted, but the shouting was all for the Lord Jesus whom he was carrying.'[3]

It would not be an exaggeration to say that Bishop Festo, although a man of international fame, was also a Ugandan patriot. He loved his own country. When Uganda gained her independence on 9 October 1962, he joined friends in the celebrations. These were held in Kampala's large stadium and included the official hand-over ceremony, numerous floats and processions, and a spectacular fireworks display. 'Festo joined in the joy and optimism of a free independent Uganda', wrote his friend and colleague Lilian Clarke. And as for the Ugandan people's formal mode of dress, 'Festo would never have thought of despising the wearing of hides and skins. "That was our custom," he said, and he was proud of it.'[4] Festo was also thankful for everything which makes Uganda the uniquely beautiful country it is – its people, its flora and fauna, its lakes and rivers, its rugged mountains and fruitful plains.

So President Idi Amin's seven-year reign of terror (1971–8) filled Festo with horror and foreboding. Not that the Church of Uganda was a stranger to persecution. On the contrary, it was born in suffering about 100 years earlier in that its first bishop (James Hannington) was martyred in 1885, while the following year a group of teen-age page boys went to their fiery death refusing to recant, and singing the praises of Jesus. Reflecting on Ugandan martyrdoms past and present, Festo wrote that 'a living church cannot be destroyed by fire or guns'.[5]

Within three months of the military coup which brought Idi Amin

**Makerere University, Uganda.**

to the presidency, imprisonment and torture, summary executions, murders and disappearances became common. And after the abortive invasion from Tanzania, Amin's personal insecurity provoked him to even worse atrocities. Law and order broke down. For example, Makerere University was raided, and about 200 students were brutally beaten up. Festo had the courage to protest, but his protest was not heeded. The leaders of the Anglican, Roman Catholic and Muslim communities then prepared a joint statement, but they were not granted an audience. Yet the church continued to grow steadily, and huge crowds crammed the churches to celebrate Christmas 1976.

The following month an estimated 30,000 people attended the consecration of Bishop Yorum Bamunoba. Many government, army and police leaders were present. Festo was the preacher. He proclaimed the gospel without fear or favour, laying his emphasis on the Cross. Then he reminded the authorities of the divine origin of their power, and challenged them not to misuse it.

The thrust of his message evidently reached the ears of the President, for six days later in the early hours of the morning Archbishop Janani Luwum's home was raided by armed men, who accused him of storing arms and insisted on searching his house. This provocative act prompted the Archbishop to summon all his bishops for a three-day consultation. They decided to prepare a thorough memorandum to the President (Festo was on the drafting committee), tabulating their grievances and protesting against the lawlessness of the regime. They then asked to see the President, but he refused. A few days later, however,

**Illustration based on a sketch by James Hannington of Ugandans inspecting his tent.**

Janani Luwum was summoned to State House in Entebbe. These two men, the President and the Archbishop, had a vigorous confrontation. The same day the memorandum to the President was handed over personally. The following day all religious leaders were summoned, and Chinese weapons were produced as supposed evidence of a plot to overthrow the government. Then the leaders were dismissed, and only the Archbishop was detained. Festo and others tried to stay with him, but were not allowed to do so. It is believed that soon after this Janani Luwum was shot dead, possibly by the hand of Idi Amin himself. It is further said that he was praying aloud for his captors when he died.

Festo spent a day trying to get permission to see the body. When all attempts had failed, several of his friends, believing that he was in imminent danger of being arrested and killed, urged him and his wife Mera to escape to safety. So they left Kampala for Kabale (a drive of 260 miles). On arrival, they were told that Amin's men had been to his house four times that day to get him. So Christians drove Festo and Mera by secondary roads towards the border. After this they walked five miles at night over the mountain across the frontier into Rwanda. They reached the top of the mountain as dawn broke. They were free. They had only just eluded their world-be captors.

For several years in Uganda, as the Amin regime deteriorated, Bishop Festo had to wrestle with his thoughts. He never lost his confidence in the sovereignty of God. At the 1975 Keswick Convention, Richard Bewes has told me, Festo said: 'Satan can roar like a lion, but he has no authority to shake the throne on which Jesus is sitting.'

Thus overcoming the temptation to unbelief, he was also tempted to

**Giraffes in Uganda.**

'hardness and bitterness' towards Amin and his agents. But how could he preach the gospel of God's love while harbouring these feelings?

The crisis came during Holy Week 1977. He describes it in his own words:

**Vervet Monkey.**

> *I had to ask for forgiveness from the Lord, and for grace to love President Amin more . . . He gave assurance of forgiveness on Good Friday, when I was one of the congregation that sat for three hours in All Souls Church in London, meditating on the redeeming love of Jesus Christ. Right there the Lord healed me, and I hurried off to tell Mera about it. This was fresh air for my tired soul. I knew I had seen the Lord and been released: love filled my heart.*[6]

On 15 April 1977 Festo wrote in *Christianity Today:*

> *I love Idi Amin. I have never been his enemy . . . Is it surprising that I love him? It shouldn't be. This is a purely Christian response to the tragic events of recent weeks. It is not weakness, nor is it cowardice. Remember Christ . . . Forgiveness is creative. Retaliation is destructive . . . Love can heal, and I will be committed to that until I die.*

After two years of exile Festo was able to return to Uganda, and he threw himself into the work of reconciliation and reconstruction. His emphasis is well summed up in a story he loved to tell:

> *One day a little girl sat watching her mother working in the kitchen. She asked her mummy, 'What does God do all day long?' For a while her mother was stumped, but then she said 'Darling, I'll tell you what God does all day long. He spends his whole day mending broken things.'*[7]

FOOTNOTES

1. Anne Coomes, *Festo Kivengere*, the authorised biography (Monarch, 1990), p. 294.
2. *Ibid.*, p. 300.
3. *Ibid.*, p. 305. See also Festo Kivengere, *I Love Idi Amin: the story of triumph under fire in the midst of suffering and persecution in Uganda* (Revell, 1977), pp. 23-24.
4. Anne Coomes, *op. cit.*, pp. 222-3.
5. Festo Kivengere, *I love Idi Amin*, p. 13.
6. *Ibid.* p. 62.
7. Anne Coomes, *op. cit.* pp. 306-307. Quoted from Festo Kivengere, *Revolutionary Love* (Kingsway, 1985), p. 60.

# Wildlife in East Africa

'Praise the LORD . . . you mountains and all hills, . . .
wild animals . . . small creatures and flying birds . . . .
Let them praise the name of the LORD.'
(Psalm 148)

*Overall*: Rhino on the plains below Mount Kilimanjaro.
*Above left to right:* Lion; Zebra; Thomson's Gazelle.
*Below*: *far left and middle*: Crested Crane, the emblem of Uganda;
*right*: Scarlet-chested Sunbird.
*Bottom*: An average-sized elephant weighs five tons and never stops eating.

# 7. Mohandas Gandhi

## *Founder of Modern India*

IT IS NOT DIFFICULT TO BE A LOVER OF INDIA. The gentleness and simplicity of its people, with their spiritual sensitivity and hunger for transcendence, its handsome men, elegant sari–clad women and vivacious children with their wondering eyes and ready laughter – these are some of the characteristics which endear Indians to those of us who have the good fortune to know any.

One cannot visit modern India without thinking

Delhi

INDIA

INDIAN OCEAN

ARABIAN SEA

SRI LANKA

**Statue of Gandhi seated, Woburn Square, London.**

MAHATMA GANDHI

of Mohandas Gandhi its founder and sensing his influence. He studied law in London and practised it for a while in South Africa. During his lifetime he threw himself successively into three struggles – for the civil rights of Indians in South Africa, for India's liberation from British rule, and for the radical transformation of Indian society. He dreamed of a new India, in which men and women would be equal, untouchables would be '*harijans*' (children of God), adherents of all religions would live together in harmony, the army would be abolished, and village life would be reconstructed. 'All his struggles', wrote George Woodcock, '. . . were concerned fundamentally with the quality of living'.[1]

Undergirding Gandhi's social vision were the two concepts of '*ahimsa*' ('refraining from harming others') and '*satyagraha*' ('truth-force', i.e. trying to win opponents by the power of truth and 'by the example of suffering willingly endured').[2] And behind both was his vision of Jesus, especially as the preacher of the Sermon on the Mount. 'It is that sermon which has endeared Jesus to me,' he wrote, 'it went straight to my heart'.[3] Moreover, he not only preached; he practised what he preached, in his willingness to suffer without retaliation. Yet he remained a Hindu all his life, unable to accept the uniqueness of Jesus Christ.

All this became vivid to me when I visited Gandhi's ashram at Sevagram, where he lived between 1936 and 1946. I saw his austere living quarters, his wooden bed, his simple toilet and his famous walking stick. There too by his bedside was the glass-fronted bookcase in which

*Above:* **Crowded market street in Delhi.**

*Above right:* **Gandhi memorial in Delhi, India.**

he kept the Bhagavad Gita, the Bible and the Koran. He loved these three books equally, he sometimes said. I wanted specially to examine his Bible, to see if he had underlined any parts of the Sermon on the Mount. But the bookcase was locked, and nobody seemed to have the key.

The famous American Methodist missionary, Dr Stanley Jones, who enjoyed Gandhi's personal friendship, once asked him how he thought Christianity could become 'naturalised' in Indian soil and no longer a foreign plant. Gandhi replied that 'Christians . . . must begin to live more like Jesus Christ', that they must practise their religion 'without adulterating or toning it down', and that they must put their 'emphasis upon love, for love is the centre and soul of Christianity'.[4]

Another Indian Hindu who stressed the primacy of love is Vinoba Bhave, who was perhaps Gandhi's longest and most faithful disciple. He founded the 'Bhoodan' movement, persuading wealthy landowners to redistribute some of their land to the landless poor. For fifteen years Vinoba walked the length and breadth of India promoting this movement. In 1981 I visited him in his ashram. It was early evening, and Vinoba was about to retire. He sat cross-legged on his bed. Now in his mid-eighties, he was thin and frail; his daily diet consisted of two glasses of milk and sixteen spoonfuls of honey. Because of his deafness my companions and I had to communicate our greetings to him in writing. Taking off his spectacles, he brought the paper close to his eyes and contemplated it with great solemnity. He then made the Indian '*namaste*'

*Top*: **The Taj Mahal, Agra.**

*Above*: **Gandhi's wooden bed at his ashram at Sevagram.**

sign of respect with both hands to each of us in turn, which we recip-rocated. Next he gave a rapid flick of his right hand, which signified unambiguously 'the audience is over, you may go now' or 'good night, I'm going to bed'.

A few years later, at a conference in Kerala, I heard an Indian church leader speak of his visit to Vinoba's ashram, shortly before he died at the age of ninety-nine. 'Have you any message for Christian churches?' he asked him. 'Yes', replied Vinoba, lifting three fingers into the air, 'first, love one another; secondly, love your neighbour as yourself, and thirdly, love your enemies'. But, as the church leader went on to comment, Indian churches are not conspicuous for their loving. Indeed, it has been said that the biggest ecumenical gathering in India is in the lawcourts, since it is there that Christians of different traditions meet, in order to prosecute and fight one another. It seems truly tragic that Indian Christians should need Hindu leaders to exhort them to love.

One of India's most eloquent Indian exhibitions of love is that mag-nificent Muslim mausoleum, the Taj Mahal. It was built in the middle of the seventeenth century, on the south bank of the River Jumna at Agra, about 125 miles south of Delhi, by the mogul emperor Shah Jahan. He intended it to be an everlasting memorial to his much-loved wife Mumtaz Mahal, who had died in childbirth. She had been his

59

**An Indian student conference proclaiming 'Jesus Christ is Lord'.**

comrade on all his journeys, his counsellor and his inspiration. So he was heartbroken when she died and determined to perpetuate her memory by building the finest sepulchre ever. 'Taj Mahal' is believed to be an abbreviation of her name. Architects and craftsmen were recruited from many countries, and more than 20,000 workmen completed the task in twenty-two years.

The Taj Mahal has been described as 'the most extravagant monument ever built for love'. Indeed, if it was an expression of love, it was also a protest against death, an attempt to defy death by preserving the memory of a mortal whom it had overcome. Love and death. We found ourselves reflecting on these things. For the fear of death and the search for love are two basic human preoccupations, two ingredients of contemporary *angst*, at least in the Western world.

Words cannot sum up the breath-taking grandeur of the Taj Mahal. Its square marble building, surmounted by its dome, stands on an extensive raised and paved platform; is framed by four tall ornamental minarets; and is set in formal gardens including a long shallow canal, in whose waters it is clearly reflected. Some friends and I were fortunate enough to arrive in the evening as the sun was setting, and to return early the following morning, before the sun had broken through the mist. The white marble, whether glowing in sunlight or shining like silver in moonlight, was deeply impressive.

Leaving the Taj, we visited a small nearby factory, in which six men, sitting on the floor, were fitting mosaic into marble, claiming that the same Muslim family, who crafted the Taj's original marble mosaic, have handed down their secret art from father to son across the centuries.

Great as were these works of men, I confess that I was now looking forward to seeing some of the works of the Lord, namely the avifauna of Bharatpur, a few miles to the west. It was originally the private shooting reserve of the local maharajas, who wantonly destroyed huge numbers of waterfowl. But now, largely through the influence of the late Salim Ali, India's most distinguished ornithologist, it is a world famous bird sanctuary, and, since 1981, the Keoladeo National Park. It consists of eleven square miles of swamp, marsh, scrub, grassland and forest, which are the home of some 350 resident and migratory bird species. The most sought-after birds of Bharatpur are the four kinds of Crane. The rarest is the Siberian Crane, but we also saw Sarus Cranes – tall, grey, stately, with bright red cheek, collar and legs. In spite of the splendour of the Taj

**A mosaic craftsman completes a marble table in Agra, near the Taj Mahal.**

Mahal, I felt like crying out: 'Great are the works of the Lord; they are pondered by all who delight in them' (Psalm 111:2).

I return now to the related themes of love and death, as illustrated in the extraordinary life of Mother Teresa. Although born in Yugoslavia, she became an Indian citizen. In his London Lectures on 'Christ and the Media' (1976), Malcolm Muggeridge took up Dean Inge's oft-quoted aphorism that 'Christianity is caught not taught' and applied it to love. 'Love is caught not taught, like a virus', he said. 'Mother Teresa is a hotbed of infection.'

I was fortunate enough to meet her in Dacca, Bangladesh, in 1981. She was there for a civic reception. So I wondered if an encounter might be possible even though (as her protectors commented ironically) 'Mother Teresa talks only to God and to prime ministers!" My friends and I were lucky, however, to be granted five minutes. I introduced myself as a friend of Malcolm Muggeridge. Her face lit up. 'He has really come to know Jesus for himself', she said. I then gave her a book, whose dust jacket included a representation of Richard Westall's *Ecce Homo*, whose original hangs on the east wall of All Souls Church, Langham Place in London. It depicts Jesus surrounded by hostile priests and soldiers. I drew Mother Teresa's attention to the fact that three human hands round the head of Jesus are pointing at him and seem to symbolize our witness to him: 'How beautiful', she murmured, and then added perceptively 'but *his* hands are tied.' 'Pray for us,' she requested, as we parted, 'that we may not spoil God's work, and that it may remain his work.' With that she left, a frail diminutive figure, dressed in a slightly soiled white sari

*Above:* Detail from Richard Westall's Ecce Homo showing the tied hands of Jesus.

*Right:* Mother Teresa of Calcutta.

edged in blue and a dark grey cardigan, the light of Christ's love shining through the creases of her wrinkled face.

In his famous book *Calcutta* Geoffrey Moorhouse refers to 'the attractive absurdity of Christian love' as an explanation of why Mother Teresa and her Missionaries of Charity carry the dying in from the pavements.

> *They have been brought here* [he writes] *because of a curious and alien philosophy . . . , unfathomable to the deepest dogmas of Hinduism, that there is some point in bringing a human being (who has been totally neglected since birth) to a place where he can die at least in a scrap of dignity, and with somebody aware of his end.*[5]

'Absurd' and 'alien' such love must seem to human calculation, but it is the love of God. Its supreme manifestation in the history of the world was in the cross of Christ. For 'God demonstrates his own love for us in this: while we were still sinners Christ died for us' (Romans 5:8)

FOOTNOTES

1. George Woodcock, *Gandhi*, Fontana Modern Masters series (Collins, 1972), p. 27.

2. *Ibid.*, p. 39.

3. *Gandhi: an autobiography: the story of my experiments with truth* (ET, Jonathan Cape, 1949), p. 58.

4. Stanley Jones, *The Christ of the Indian Road* (1925; Hodder and Stoughton, 1926), pp. 146-8.

5. Geoffrey Moorhouse, *Calcutta* (Weidenfeld and Nicolson, 1971), p. 82.

# Birds of India

**Top right**: Little Green Bee-eater.
**Middle**: Lesser Indian Kingfisher.
**Bottom left**: Peacock in display.
**Bottom right**: Sarus Cranes.

# 8. Lily O'Hanlon and Hilda Steele
## *Patient Pioneers in Nepal*

I HAD THE PLEASURE OF MEETING BOTH Hilda Steele and Lily O'Hanlon in January 1975 in Nepal, and at once I knew that they were special. Intrepid, indomitable, indefatigable might be appropriate epithets. Only gradually, however, did I come to learn the full story of these patient pioneers of mission.

They had met first in 1931 in London, when Hilda was a Bible College student and Pat (as Lily was always known to her friends) was a newly qualified doctor. Their second meeting took place in 1933 at language school in Landour, North India. After a day of prayer and fasting they found that they were kindred spirits. Both were strong characters and visionaries, women of faith and of prayer. And both had Nepal written on their hearts.

Nepal has always been shrouded with an aura of mystery. Geographically

**Lily O'Hanlon and Hilda Steele.**

***Above:* Sunrise on Annapurna.**

isolated and even inaccessible, wedged between Tibet to the north and India to the south, cut off by the huge Himalayan range along its northern border, its many tribes of Mongolian origin forming a rich cultural tapestry, Nepal is 5,000 square miles of hills and valleys, rivers and forests.

It has also had a long and turbulent history, including a special relationship with Britain, coming under British protection in 1815. Its highly trained Gurkha regiments in the Indian army won high acclaim during the world wars of the twentieth century. But in 1846 the infamous regime of the Rana families began. Their leaders established a brutal autocracy, demoted the king to a powerless puppet, reserved the influential political positions for themselves, recruited large numbers of slaves, and lived luxuriously in their palaces. In addition, their foreign policy was to keep the country impervious to alien influences. Millions of citizens left the country of their own free will; Nepali Christians were not even allowed to stay. So Nepal was a closed country. Would it ever again open to the gospel? Humanly speaking, it looked extremely unlikely. But the unfolding events tell a marvellous story of divine providence.

Before returning to the Rana regime with its iron clamp on the country, we need to consider the beginning of another story, in 1933,

**A Nepali boy.**

although the two appear at first to be unconnected. Pat O'Hanlon describes herself at that time as 'a very new missionary in the Ludhiana Medical College' (in North India). On New Year's Day 1933 she believed that God gave her the promise of Deuteronomy 11:11, which reads: 'The land whither ye go to possess it is a land of hills and valleys'.[1] She interpreted the 'land of hills and valleys' as referring to Nepal, and she and Hilda Steele clung to this promise for sixteen long years, from November 1936 to November 1952.

They took up residence in a little village called Nautanwa, India, four miles south of the border with Nepal. When they arrived, they had no house, no friends and no language. But they could see that Nautanwa was a strategic link between India and Nepal, with thousands of merchants and pilgrims passing through every year.

During those sixteen years of anxious, prayerful waiting, the two lady missionaries were far from inactive. They learned all they could about Nepali language and culture; they opened a school for boys, a sewing class for girls, and a dispensary for both residents and travellers; they sold gospels, showed magic lantern slides, and arranged Sunday services. They also began to build up a small team of Christian Nepalis, who would enter the country with them when the time came. Thus the Nepal Evangelistic Band was born, a band 'whose hearts God had touched' (1 Samuel 10:26).

It is now that the two stories (the political and the missionary) interconnect. In 1950, after just more than a century of Rana rule, it was overthrown in a revolution, the king was reinstated, and new freedoms were promised. Was this the divine signal the missionaries were waiting for? Was the door beginning to open at last? It seemed so.

That same year (1950) Pat O'Hanlon and Hilda Steele received out of the blue an invitation from Sir Christopher Summerhayes, the first and newly appointed British ambassador to Nepal, and Lady Summerhayes, to visit them for a holiday in Katmandu. Summerhayes is a somewhat unusual surname, and Pat O'Hanlon remembered that the games mistress at her school had been a Miss Summerhayes, who turned out to be the Ambassador's sister.

While the missionaries were staying in the British Embassy, on Nepali soil at last, the Ambassador arranged for them to meet the Health Minister and even the Prime Minister, so that they could submit their application to build a hospital in Pokhara, about 100 miles north-west of Katmandu. During the next months their appli-

**A plaque designed to educate Nepalis in public health.**

**Some of the pupils of the boys' school run by Hilda (*left*) and Lily (*right*) in front of the missionaries' home in Nautanwa before they entered Nepal.**

cation was refused (in spite of the Health Minister's affability), then granted on conditions, then cancelled a week later, and finally given. During this cat-and-mouse activity the missionaries continued to cling to the promises of God which, they remembered, are not inherited by faith alone but 'by faith *and patience*' (Hebrews 6:12).

The day soon came for the little Christian party, who had waited sixteen years for this moment, to cross the frontier and, as it were, 'possess' the land of hills and valleys. There were eleven of them – six missionaries (including two doctors and three nurses) and five Nepali Christians (including Pastor David Mukhia and his wife Premi). They needed nineteen coolies to carry all their baggage, and the journey took them a week.

Soon after their arrival in Pokhara they built three huts of bamboo and thatch, which enabled them at once to open a dispensary and to treat a steadily increasing number of needy patients. But they had to battle with wind and rain, storm and flood, so that they decided to replace their home-made huts with prefabricated aluminium ones. It was the sun's reflections on the aluminium which won for the buildings the name 'The Shining Hospital'. A notable event of those early years was the official visit of King Mahendra in 1961, in order to open

**Nepalis at market.**    the operating theatre.

The International Nepal Fellowship (as the Nepal Evangelistic Band was now named) also responded to the enormous unmet needs of leprosy sufferers. The government 'leper colonies' kept them isolated from the community, but gave them no treatment and no hope; they eked out a miserable existence in squalor and despair. It was wonderful, therefore, when the INF obtained fifteen acres of land and on it constructed the 'Green Pastures' leprosarium.

It had already been opened more than fifteen years when I paid my privileged visit to Nepal in 1975 as the guest of the United Mission to Nepal. Having flown in to Katmandu, I was driven to Pokhara along the winding mountain road, which had recently been built by the Chinese, through small villages and past paddy fields on terraced hillsides. I was struck by the neat land cultivation, the absence of litter, and the people's sense of humour and of colour. Three quarters of the way to our destination, when we turned a corner, the distant snow-capped Himalayan peaks came into spectacular view, washed pink by the setting sun. The whole Annapurna range is seen from Pokhara, and in particular Machapuchare or Fish-Tail at 23,000 feet, which was to form the backdrop of our lives that week.

Apart from speaking to the mission workers' conference morning and evening, I was free in the middle of the day, while the conference was in business session. I loved to walk along the River Seti or Sheti ('white' from its foaming mountain waters). A pair of Brown Dippers were feeding their young. The Brown Dipper is found in fast-flowing rivers throughout northern Asia from Siberia to Japan. Its name is derived from its strange habit of standing on mid-river rocks and 'dipping' or curtseying to the world at large.

Both the UMN (United Mission to Nepal) and the INF

*Above*: **Brown Dipper near Pokhara.**
*Below*: **Sunrise at Fish-tail Mountain.**

**A Nepali village.**

(International Nepal Fellowship) now have a contract with the government, which has to be re-negotiated regularly. The concept of a government-mission partnership should be of increasing mutual benefit. On the one hand, the missions are collaborating with the government's programmes for agriculture, education and medicine. They are helping to build and staff hospitals and schools, and are involved in a technical training institute and a plywood factory. The community health programme included instruction in personal hygiene, nutrition, clean water, mother and baby clinics, and both TB and leprosy control. I saw some of this in operation, and was immensely impressed by what I saw.

On the other hand, as the missions support government programmes, we hope and pray that the government will grant freedom to churches and missions. Nepal is a signatory of the 1948 UN Declaration of Human Rights, which includes freedom to profess, practise, propagate and change one's religion. To change one's religion in Nepal, however, is still illegal and carries quite severe penalties of imprisonment. Yet the church soldiers on and refuses to be intimidated. It continues to testify to Jesus Christ, and to the love, joy and peace which he gives to his followers.

But now, as I write in 2002, the political situation is extremely volatile. The nation is mourning the assassination of the much-loved

**Nepali woman near Pokhara.**

**The valley of the river Seti.**

King Birendra and most of the royal family; the Maoist guerrilla movement is challenging the ruling Nepali Congress party; and people see on the horizon the awful spectre of civil war.

Yet the church of Jesus Christ in Nepal, although persecuted, continues to grow. It has had indigenous leadership from the beginning, and it is reckoned that there are now about 20,000 baptized Christians in some 200 congregations, all springing from that providential opening of the door in 1952.

FOOTNOTE

1. Lily O'Hanlon, *Into Nepal* (International Nepal Fellowship Publications, 1974), p. 2. See also *At the Foot of the Fish-Tail Mountain* by Lily M. O'Hanlon (privately published, 1957).

# 9. Hudson Taylor
## *Penetrating Inland China*

I T WAS WHILE I WAS AN UNDERGRADUATE AT CAMBRIDGE University that I discovered the literary genre called 'Christian Biography', tales of great Christian leaders from the past. Some of the first I devoured told the story of Hudson Taylor, the nineteenth century pioneer missionary in inland China. I began with the hefty standard volume entitled *Hudson Taylor in Early Years* (1912) by his son and daughter-in-law, Howard and Mary Taylor. Next came a more popular paperback, *Hudson Taylor: the Man Who Believed God* (1929), by Marshall Broomhall, Howard Taylor's cousin. Later still John Pollock wrote his candid portrait, *Hudson Taylor and Maria* (1962). At different times and in different ways these books brought Hudson

**Junk in Kowloon harbour.**

Taylor to life in my mind, and he became something of a hero to me.

My admiration for Hudson Taylor inevitably gave me a long-standing interest in China. So when I received an official invitation from the China Christian Council to visit its four leading seminaries in 1996, I did not hesitate to accept. At the same time, I approached my visit with the due modesty with which all visitors from the west should come, on account of China's enormous dimensions. First, we remember China's long history, many dynasties and artistic achievements, going back to the time before Europe even existed. Secondly, we remember China's vast territory, compared with which Europe appears hardly bigger than a postage-stamp! Thirdly, we recall China's huge population, comprising almost one-fifth of the entire human race. We Europeans cannot compete with these statistics.

But I also approached China with some degree of understanding of the history of its church during the second half of the twentieth century. Perhaps I should remind my readers of one or two salient dates. 1949 is commemorated in China as the year of 'liberation', when the Communists won their victory over the nationalist forces. The following year a group of Christian leaders asked premier Chou En-Lai for the legal protection of the Christian minority. Chou replied that the heart of the people would not be won by law, but only

**Street in Kowloon, Hong Kong.**

**An elderly Chinese villager.**

if the church purged itself of foreign influences and became authentically Chinese. This reminded the leaders of the 'three self' principle which the church had known about since 1905. They may not have known that it had already been promulgated half a century earlier in relation to African churches by Henry Venn of Britain's Church Missionary Society. He wrote in 1851 of 'the settlement of a Native Church under Native pastors upon a self-supporting, self-governing and self-extending system'. Roland Allen also, who was an Anglican missionary in North China from 1895 to 1903, wrote eloquently about the same vision in his well known books *Missionary Methods: St Paul's or Ours?* (1912) and *The Spontaneous Expansion of the Church* (1927). At all events the church leaders in China reported back to Chou, and in 1950 the 'Three Self Patriotic Movement' was born, to ensure that the church would be self-governing, self-financing and self-propagating.

We jump now to 1966 and the outbreak of the so-called 'Cultural Revolution'. The Red Guards went on the rampage. Churches were desecrated and closed. Bibles and Christian books were confiscated and burned. Religious leaders were imprisoned, tortured and sent to re-education camps. This reign of terror lasted a whole decade.

The year 1979 is celebrated, however, as the beginning of the 'opening up', initiated by Deng Shao-Ping. Christians were now allowed to assemble again. Churches were re-opened. Leaders were re-instated. Also the China Christian Council came into operation on

**A Chinese market.**

**Chairman Mao.**

two principles – (1) the Three Self Patriotic Movement and its rejection of foreign interference, and (2) 'mutual respect'. Having deliberately moved into a 'post-denominational' era, churches could choose their own mode of baptism, eucharistic liturgy and styles of worship.

I find it hard to evaluate my two visits to China in 1996 and 1999, and especially the relations between church and government, freedom and control, registered and unregistered churches. On the one hand, I had no sense of personal restriction, no fear of being followed or watched, and no knowledge of any informers. On the contrary, I felt entirely free, although of course it was taken for granted that in my sermons I would not say anything against the regime. The church services I attended were most impressive. Take as an example the Chong Wen Men church in Beijing, which was formerly Methodist. The congregation overflowed into the basement and the courtyard, listening by closed-circuit television, and is said to have totalled over 2,000 people. I was besieged afterwards by autograph hunters. Then a group of young people gathered round. 'I'm a new believer', said one, and 'I've been a believer for a month, but have not yet been baptized', said another. Next a flood of questions was let loose. 'How soon should a new believer be baptized?' 'What happens if I sin again?' 'How can I learn to pray?' 'Should I give up smoking and drinking?' 'Can I pray lying on my back?' 'What should I do to succeed in the Christian life?' It was wonderful to witness their spiritual hunger, their enthusiasm, and their freedom to ask questions.

On the other hand, freedom remains limited in China. All the media (newspapers, radio and television) are strictly controlled. Although the unregistered house churches are not really 'underground', yet they also are not free. They are free to preach, but only in churches, and only if not criticizing the government. They are free to evangelize, but only in church buildings. Bibles are now available. The Amity Press produced fourteen million copies during its first ten years of operation, and is now publishing about five million a year. But Bibles are not allowed to be sold in secular bookshops, only at specified distribution centres. It is for infringing these petty regulations that house church pastors continue to be arrested and imprisoned, or for maintaining contact with overseas churches. And all the time the terrible massacre of protesting students in Tiananmen Square, Beijing, in 1989 is a warning of the government's resolve, if provoked, to crack down ruthlessly on any further pro-democracy demonstrations.

Through all these ups and downs the church continues to grow. Tony Lambert writes in his book *The Resurrection of the Chinese Church* (1991):

> The phenomenal growth of the Church in China since the Cultural Revolution is one of the miracles of twentieth century Church history. The evidence is now massive. The Party is so concerned about the phenomenon that it has coined the phrase 'Christianity fever' . . . to describe it.[1]

Tony Lambert goes on to give evidence that the total number of Protestant Christians, registered and unregistered, was by 1989 about twenty million.[2] He adds: 'the lives and deaths of the martyrs have borne much fruit'.[3]

The multiplication of believers in China, which has taken place *after* the withdrawal of foreign missionaries, is without doubt a work of the Holy Spirit, and is beyond Hudson Taylor's wildest dreams. So let me return to him.

I would like to share with you the memorable story of his conver-

**The earliest party of CIM missionaries on board the ship *Lammermuir*.**

sion, and then focus on particular lessons about faith which I have learned from him.

First, his conversion. Born in 1832 into a godly home in Yorkshire, during his adolescence Hudson Taylor's spiritual interests grew cold and he developed materialistic ambitions. His mother and elder sister began to pray earnestly for his conversion. When he was seventeen years old, during a holiday afternoon, while rummaging about in his father's library for something to read, he found a gospel tract and began to read it 'in an utterly unconcerned frame of mind'.

Meanwhile, unknown to him, seventy or eighty miles away, his mother was experiencing an intense yearning for the conversion of her son, and persevered in prayer until she received an assurance that her prayers had been answered. While she was praying, Hudson was reading the tract. As he did so, he was arrested by the expression 'the finished work of Christ'. He asked himself what this meant.

> *Immediately the words 'it is finished' suggested themselves to my mind. What was finished? And I at once replied, 'A full and perfect atonement and satisfaction for sin': the debt was paid by the Substitute; Christ died for our sins . . . Then came the thought, 'If the whole work was finished and the whole debt paid, what is there left for me to do?' And with this dawned the joyful conviction, as light was flashed into my soul by the Holy Spirit, that there was nothing in the world to be done but to fall down on one's knees, and accepting this Saviour and his salvation, to praise him for evermore. Thus while my dear mother was praising God on her knees in her chamber, I was praising him in the old warehouse to which I had gone alone to read at my leisure this little book.*[4]

While he was still in his later teens, and now a medical student, God laid China on his heart, and specially its closed interior. He read books about China and studied the Chinese language. Then in 1853 he set sail on his four and a half month voyage to Shanghai. In 1860 he was invalided home, but his burden for inland China, far from lessening, grew heavier. One Sunday morning in June 1865 he was worshipping in a church in Brighton.

*As the full congregation rose to sing the last hymn, Taylor looked around. Pew upon pew of prosperous bearded merchants, shopkeepers, visitors; demure wives in bonnets and crinolines, scrubbed children trained to hide their impatience; the atmosphere of smug piety sickened him. He seized his hat and left. 'Unable to bear the sight of a congregation of a thousand or more Christians rejoicing in their own security, while millions were perishing for lack of knowledge, I wandered out on the sands alone, in great spiritual agony.' That Sunday morning, on Brighton's almost deserted beach, Hudson Taylor 'prayed for twenty-four willing skilful labourers'.*[5]

**Hudson Taylor as a young man.**

God answered his prayer. Having failed to find a mission agency to support him, he founded the China Inland Mission (later the Overseas Missionary Fellowship). The following year, accompanied by twenty-two missionaries, he sailed back to China, and under his dynamic leadership the mission grew steadily. By the time he died in 1905, the CIM was an international mission with 825 missionaries and more than 500 national workers, who were witnessing to Christ in all eighteen provinces of China.

Hudson Taylor's primary principle was 'dependence on God alone'. It was not an accident, therefore, that Marshall Broomhall entitled his biography *The Man Who Believed God*. Whether as a Cambridge student or later as an ordained pastor, I have been challenged by Hudson Taylor to a greater and wiser faith. He seems to me to exemplify a robust, reasonable and realistic faith. In particular he has taught me four important aspects of Christian faith.

**Hudson Taylor with his wife Maria.**

First, *faith rests on God's faithfulness.* I remember reading that Hudson Taylor liked to render Jesus' command 'have faith in God' (Mark 11:22) with the words 'reckon on the faithfulness of God'. This paraphrase, although not exegetically exact, is theologically correct. Human faith and divine faithfulness are the obverse and reverse of the same coin. It is precisely because God is faithful that faith is reasonable, for there is no more trustworthy person than God. So to trust the trustworthy is hardly daring or adventurous; it is plain, sober common sense.[6]

Secondly, *faith is the trust of a child.* God is not only the Faithful One, but our Father too through Jesus Christ. He invites us to call him 'Father' and to share our concerns and needs with him as children do with their parents. I cannot do better here than quote Hudson Taylor himself:

> *I am taking my children with me, and I notice that it is not difficult for me to remember that the little ones need breakfast in the morning, dinner at midday, and something before they go to bed at night. Indeed, I could not forget it. And I find it impossible to suppose that our Heavenly Father is less tender or mindful than I.*

Again,

*I do not believe that our Heavenly Father will ever forget his children.
I am a very poor father, but it is not my habit to forget my children.
God is a very, very good Father. It is not his habit to forget his
children.*[7]

Thirdly, *faith is as necessary in the material realm as in the spiritual*, e.g.
when needing money as much as when seeking converts. One of
Hudson Taylor's best-known aphorisms was: 'God's work done in
God's way will never lack supplies.'[8] There is a measure of debate
about what constitutes a 'faith mission', and whether financial needs
should be made known to God alone or may be disclosed to God's
people also. Certainly the apostle Paul saw nothing incongruous in
urging the Greek churches to contribute to the collection which he
was organizing for the poverty-stricken Judean churches. But under-
lying his appeal was his confidence in God.

During the last two decades All Souls Church, Langham Place in
London, has had to face two daunting and unavoidable building projects. Michael Baughen (later Bishop of Chester) led us in the first and
Richard Bewes (our current Rector) in the second. And though the
two leaders have differed from one another in style, they have been
united in faith. It is from Hudson Taylor as much as from anybody else
that I myself have learned the secondary importance of money.
I believe strongly that if we are doing God's work according to God's
will in God's way, the necessary money will be forthcoming.

Fourthly, *faith is not incompatible with the use of means*. On his first
voyage to China in 1853, the vessel in which Hudson Taylor was
sailing was caught in a severe storm, off the coast of Wales. He had
promised his mother that he would wear a life-belt. But when the
captain ordered passengers to put them on, he felt it would be a sign
of unbelief and thereby dishonouring to God. So he gave his away. But
as he reflected on his action, he came to see his mistake. 'The use of
means', he wrote, 'ought not to lessen our faith in God, and our faith
in God ought not to hinder our using whatever means he has given
us for the accomplishment of his own purposes.'[9] Similarly, we might
add, a farmer's trust in God is not incompatible with ploughing,
sowing and reaping, nor a patient's with going to the doctor and
taking medicine, nor a church leader's with necessary organization.
Indeed, when means are available but neglected, faith becomes pre-

**Changsha, capital of Hunan, where Hudson Taylor died.**

sumption. A contemporary example is provided by the so-called *kufu-fuka* (Swahili for 're-awakening') in Uganda. This revival group rejects as sinful the insurance of property and its protection by guard dogs because (in their view) it would mean putting their trust in dogs rather than in God.

To sum up, authentic faith is not a synonym for superstition or credulity or lazy inactivity. It rests on the faithfulness and the fatherliness of God, and is accompanied by sensible precautions and actions.

FOOTNOTES

1. *op. cit.* (Hodder and Stoughton, 1991), p. 142.

2. *op. cit.*, pp. 143-146.

3. *op. cit.*, pp. 267-8.

4. Marshall Broomhall, *op. cit.*, pp. 23-25

5. *Hudson Taylor and Maria*, pp. 113-4.

6. Hudson Taylor wrote: "'Hold God's faithfulness" Mark 11:22. Such we believe to be the purport of the three (Greek) words of our Lord . . . rendered "Have faith in God" . . .' (*China's Millions*, Vol. I, No. 5, November 1875, p. 55).

7. Marshall Broomhall, *The Man Who Believed God* (CIM, 1929), pp. 138-139.

8. Quoted by John Pollock in *Hudson Taylor and Maria* (Hodder and Stoughton, 1962), pp. 17-18.

9. Marshall Broomhall, *op. cit.*, pp. 52-53.

# 10. Paul White
## *Australian Jungle Doctor*

I COUNT MYSELF EXTREMELY FORTUNATE to have visited Australia at least ten times – the land of aromatic gum trees, of rolling countryside and rain forest, of sun, sand and surf, of colourful parrots flying swiftly through the trees, as if the Garden of Eden were still our home, of koalas and kangaroos, and of the laughter or cackle (according to one's mood) of the noisy Kookaburra.

But whom should I choose as our teacher in that vast territory? I could have selected one of the last six Archbishops of Sydney, all of whom I have had the privilege of knowing personally. But all but the first two (Howard Mowll and Hugh Gough) are still alive as I write. So I have chosen Paul White, who for many years was known world-wide as 'The Jungle

Northern Territory

**AUSTRALIA**

Queensland

Western Australia

South Australia

**Sydney Harbour Bridge, with the famous Opera House beyond.**

Doctor'. Not many people are able to write *two* autobiographies. But Paul did – the first entitled *Doctor of Tanganyika* (1941) and the second *Alias Jungle Doctor* (1977).

Paul White's jungle doctor reputation was based on his three heroic years in charge of Mvumi hospital, twenty miles from Dodoma, which is now the capital of Tanzania. Mvumi was the base hospital, and from it Paul White supervised six other hospitals throughout the country. He was the only doctor for a quarter of a million people.

When he arrived at Mvumi with his wife Mary and their baby son David (Rosemary their daughter was born later), the odds stacked against them were enormous. There was no electricity; there were only hurricane lamps. There was no running water; water had to be brought in kerosene tins from the nearest well a mile away. The hospital was woefully ill-equipped, with a makeshift theatre, and kettles for sterilizers. Only later did the local people, under Paul White's supervision, build a new hospital, with path. lab, dispensary, theatre, maternity ward and men's ward, all for £400.

In addition to shortages, they had to contend with white ants, cockroaches and snakes. As for medical conditions, the variety would be enough to challenge any doctor.

*There were skin diseases by the score, deep, stinking ulcers, heavily infected scabies, angry thorn-wounds; lepers infectious and non-*

*infectious. . . . There were paralysed children, and eye cases of all kinds. I saw mere babies with scarred, sightless eyes, the result of a witch-doctor's treatment; others had eyes matted with pus and swarming with flies. Old folk with cataracts were led in by their relatives. Malaria cases, bundled up in blankets, sat shivering in the hot sun. Then came a series of minor ailments . . . , and lastly those who would like to taste my medicine.*[1]

Worst of all was the nefarious influence of the witch-doctors and of the old women their accomplices. Their superstitious practices and prejudices were extremely hard to combat. The most dreadful example was the infant mortality rate due to neglect, maltreatment and infanticide. Horrified by 'the stark tragedy of African motherhood and child life',[2] Paul White kept careful statistics. He discovered that in one year 780 out of 1,000 babies born in the bush died before their first birthday, whereas the number born to mothers who had been educated in the local Christian school was reduced to 190.

Paul wrote that 'one needs the wisdom of Solomon and the patience of Job', and he seems to have been given both in abundant measure, for, he added, 'one cannot drag people from the Stone Age into the twentieth century in a few short months'.[3]

Gradually, however, he made solid progress. He gathered round him a team of skilled and faithful helpers. The hold of the witch-doctors began to relax. Gradually too people learned from community health talks the elementary truths of nutrition and hygiene, even if they preserved the picturesque sayings of their own language, describing indigestion (for example) as 'having a restless snake inside them'.

**The kangaroo, indissolubly linked with Australia.**

In what little time he could snatch from his medical ministry, Paul managed to learn both Swahili and Chigogo, although in the early stages he made some hilarious mistakes, like telling the parable of the five wise kettles and the five foolish ones. He kept his own sense of humour, laughing at our ludicrous human vagaries.

Above all, his compassion was a true mirror of the love of God for sinners like us. It enabled him to proclaim with authenticity that this loving God forgives sins, takes away the fear of death and fills our lives with abundant life and joy.

Back in Australia Paul White specialized in rheumatology. But at the same time he plunged without reserve into numerous Australian and international Christian ministries. For two years he was Home Secretary of the Church Missionary Society (NSW), and for six years

**Paul White with a Gogo warrior.**

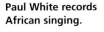

**Paul White records African singing.**

Honorary General Secretary of the Inter Varsity Fellowship, which later became the Australian Fellowship of Evangelical Students (AFES). During this time he united the student movement which had been seriously divided, he increased membership, he laid a strong emphasis on mission, and he reinstated the Annual Conference. Later he was three times elected President of AFES. He was also active in his church, in Scripture Union and the Crusaders' Union, and Chairman of African Enterprise (Australia) from 1979 to 1991.

From the 1940s onwards Paul's literary output exploded. His seventy-eight books between them were translated into 109 languages. He also moved into radio, being broadcast on forty-five Australian stations. He was a born raconteur, filling his stories with African colour and adventure, and he held his audiences spellbound. He summed up his technique in five stages: 'Hook 'em, hold 'em, hang on to 'em, humour 'em and hit 'em', the last being the crucial punch-line. With gifted artists as colleagues he then branched out into the visual field – into comics, cartoons, filmstrips, posters and videos.

Paul White could justly be described as a 'fair dinkum Aussie'. His authentic Australian accent, his outspokenness, his dislike of 'tall poppies' (socially arrogant people), his ready use of common

A Lilac-breasted Roller, one of East Africa's most spectacular birds, and a favourite of Paul White's.

Australian slang (e.g. 'a beaut bloke' or 'a bonzer kid') and his invention of his own slang, like 'BWWs', meaning 'Blokes Worth Watching', entered on a page of his prayer list as potential leaders – these and other characteristics marked him out as a genuine Australian.

None of this slang was even to the slightest degree malicious, however. He once told his friend Clifford Warne that he would never join the 'Vinegar Club', 'vinegar' being an acronym for such sour attitudes as Vindictiveness, Ill-will, Nastiness, Envy, Gossip, Anger and Resentfulness'. All these were entirely foreign to his nature.

But he did enjoy a little innocent leg-pulling. In August 1950 Paul was in Cambridge for the inaugural conference of the International Fellowship of Evangelical Students, which was being chaired by the renowned Dr D. Martyn Lloyd-Jones. Paul was met on arrival by Oliver Barclay, Assistant General Secretary of the British IVF, and sat down to lunch opposite Dr Martyn Lloyd-Jones. The following conversation ensued:

D.M.Ll.J. *'After lunch we will all go to Ely, where we will see a magnificent equestrian statue of Oliver Cromwell.'*

P.W. *(with an innocent expression) 'Oliver Barclay I know, but who is this Oliver Cromwell? Is he also in the IVF?'*

**A Sulphur-crested Cockatoo, one of Australia's 55 parrots.**

D.M.Ll.J. *(rapping the table) 'Colossal ignorance, even in a colonial!'*

*Paul went on with his lunch, but soon felt Dr Lloyd-Jones' eyes boring into his soul. He looked up and caught Dr Lloyd-Jones' eye.*

D.M.Ll.J. *'Humph! I see.'*

*The great man had never been known to have his leg pulled before; Paul had done it in the first five minutes, and lived to tell the tale.*[5]

**Colourful Australian Bottlebrush shrub.**

Although Paul was sanguine in temperament and buoyant in spirit, he had more than his fair share of suffering. His beloved wife Mary was afflicted first with severe clinical depression, then with breast cancer and finally with premature senile dementia, while he himself was a life-long victim of asthma. He knew what it was to walk through the valley of the shadow. Mary died in 1970, and some time later he married Ruth, who gave him twenty-one years of conjugal happiness.

'Some things seem to be tied up in our genes', wrote Paul White in his autobiography, and continued: 'Hamilton Hume, great-great-uncle, was quite an authority on the birds of the Australian bush'.[6] Whether bird watching is a genetic or a cultural inheritance, I share it with Paul White. Here is his eulogy of this recreation:

*It is a magnificent way of relaxing to walk through the bush and listen*

Koala.

*to the sound of Cuckoos, Whistlers, Warblers, the harmony of small birds and the concerto of the bush at sunrise and sunset. There is nothing more peaceful to a busy mind than to sit back and to listen to a dawn chorus of birds.[7]*

Then, with the advent of tape recorders, Paul White found a new way of expressing his hobby, namely by recording bird sounds. On 'one notable day', he wrote, near the Hawkesbury River north of Sydney, he recorded for forty minutes non-stop the resonant song of 'that master of mimicry and music, the Superb Lyrebird'.[8] On another 'notable day' Paul and Ruth kindly drove me to the Barren Grounds National Park, south-west of Wollongong. Our goal was to see the Swamp Parrot. Because it is a shy, nocturnal ground parrot which, at the approach of danger, prefers to run than to fly, it is seldom seen. Paul and I followed a trail through tall grass, reeds, bottle brush bushes and dwarf wattles. It was raining, and bird watching from under an umbrella is uncomfortable, to say the least. Unfortunately, Paul's asthma was making him 'puffed'. So he returned to base, and left me to fend for myself. I turned off the trail and plunged downhill into the swamp. Squelch! Squelch! I tried as methodically as possible to quarter the area, when suddenly there was a noise of whirring wings, as a long-tailed green parrot broke cover about ten yards away, flew about thirty yards low over the undergrowth, and dived for cover again. Its rapid noisy wing beat, interspersed with bouts of gliding on down-curved wings, and its quick disappearance in the bush again – were all diagnostic. We dried out over a fire, consumed a steak barbecue under our umbrellas and after lunch all managed to catch a sight of the bird we were questing.

On another occasion, when we were together at an international conference in Switzerland, Paul was taken ill and had to retire to bed. It was of course extremely disappointing for him, and his friends began to talk rather ominously about stress and overwork. I decided to pay him a pastoral visit, and wondered what verse of Scripture I could share with him, which might be appropriate and helpful. Remembering the pressure he was under, I chose Hebrews 12:12, 13 (RSV) and read:

*Therefore lift your drooping hands and strengthen your weak knees, and make straight (i.e. level) paths for your feet, so that what is lame may not be put out of joint but rather be healed.*

*Above*: **Aboriginal girl.**

*Right*: **Crimson Rosella.**

It is evident that three parts of our human anatomy are mentioned in this text – our hands, our knees and our feet, and that all three are often disabled. Our hands are 'drooping', our knees are 'weak', and our feet are 'lame'. What is particularly noteworthy, however, is that the treatment prescribed for these conditions is the same for the first and the second, but quite different for the third. If our hands are drooping, we must lift them up, and if our knees are weak we must strengthen or brace them. But if, more seriously, our feet are lame, we are not told to do anything to our feet, but rather to make level paths on which our lame feet will be able to walk. Just so, it is often right to tell people to pull themselves together. But in more serious circumstances we should rather urge them to live within their abilities and not try to stretch themselves beyond reasonable limits. Paul smiled. There was (as always) a twinkle in his eye and a dimple in his cheek. I think he got the point. But whether he changed his lifestyle is another question altogether!

Sir Marcus Loane, a former Archbishop of Sydney, gave the eulogy at Paul White's Memorial Service on 24 December 1992. He chose words with which Jesus described John the Baptist:

*He was a burning and a shining light: and you were willing for a season to rejoice in his light (John 3:35, AV).*

Affirming that Paul White's name deserved to be held in high honour, Sir Marcus concluded as follows:

*There can be no true light without both burning and shining. The wick must burn if the lamp is to shine . . . What is a candle made for, but to burn so that it will shine? So it was with John the Baptist. So it was with Paul White.*

**Top:** Australian Shelduck, also known as Mountain Duck.

***Above:*** Rainbow Lorikeet, Currumbin, Queensland.

FOOTNOTES

1. Paul White, *Doctor of Tanganyika* (1941; revised and enlarged edition Paternoster, 1952), p. 10.

2. *Ibid.*, p. 102.

3. *Ibid.*, p. 129.

4. *Alias Jungle Doctor*, p. 129.

5. This anecdote was recorded by Archbishop Sir Marcus Loane in *Men to Remember* (Acorn Press, 1987), p. 114.

6. *Alias Jungle Doctor*, p. 187

7. *Ibid*, p 105.

8. *Ibid.*, p. 193.

# Some Australian Birds

*Overall*: Black Swan in flight.

*Top right*: Lyrebird, Sherbrooke Forest.

*Above right*: King Parrot, Katoomba.

*Right*: Rainbow Bird, or Australian Bee-eater.

*Far right*: Nesting Black Swans.

# 11. Ernest Shackleton

## *Antarctic Explorer*

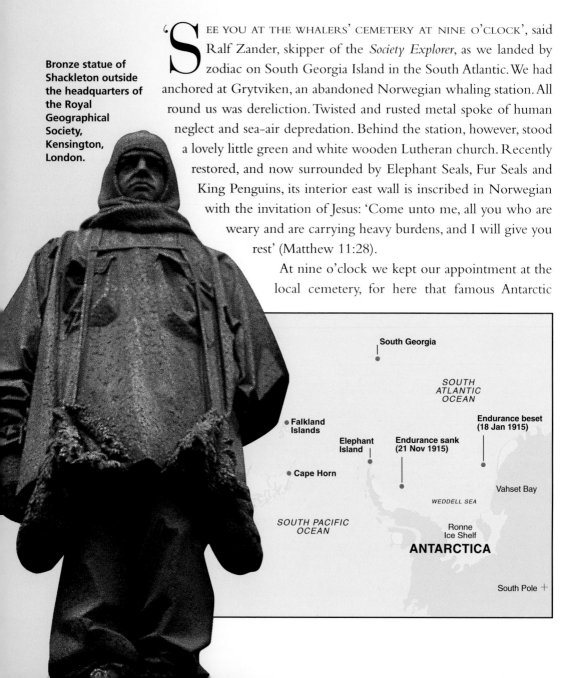

**Bronze statue of Shackleton outside the headquarters of the Royal Geographical Society, Kensington, London.**

'SEE YOU AT THE WHALERS' CEMETERY AT NINE O'CLOCK', said Ralf Zander, skipper of the *Society Explorer*, as we landed by zodiac on South Georgia Island in the South Atlantic. We had anchored at Grytviken, an abandoned Norwegian whaling station. All round us was dereliction. Twisted and rusted metal spoke of human neglect and sea-air depredation. Behind the station, however, stood a lovely little green and white wooden Lutheran church. Recently restored, and now surrounded by Elephant Seals, Fur Seals and King Penguins, its interior east wall is inscribed in Norwegian with the invitation of Jesus: 'Come unto me, all you who are weary and are carrying heavy burdens, and I will give you rest' (Matthew 11:28).

At nine o'clock we kept our appointment at the local cemetery, for here that famous Antarctic

South Georgia

SOUTH
ATLANTIC
OCEAN

Falkland
Islands

Endurance beset
(18 Jan 1915)

Elephant
Island

Endurance sank
(21 Nov 1915)

Cape Horn

Vahset Bay

WEDDELL SEA

SOUTH PACIFIC
OCEAN

Ronne
Ice Shelf

**ANTARCTICA**

South Pole +

*Above*: **Lutheran church, Grytviken, South Georgia.**

*Below*: **The inscription of Matthew 11:28 in the Grytviken church.**

explorer Ernest Shackleton is buried. Captain Zander read out a brief tribute to him as the greatest of all seamen and leaders. Then, however strange it may sound in relation to a man long dead, we drank his toast in red wine out of tiny plastic cups – a kind of secular communion service.

Ernest Shackleton was born in 1874 in County Kildare, Ireland. His father was a doctor, but he from his earliest years had had a hunger for exploration and the sea. So he became apprenticed to the Merchant Navy at the age of sixteen.

Before his epic adventure in the Antarctic, for which he is known and honoured throughout the world, he had been on two south polar expeditions, the first on the *Discovery* as part of Robert Scott's National Antarctic Expedition (1901-1903), and the second which reached within 100 miles of the South Pole (1908-1909). For this exploit he was knighted.

When Roald Amundsen, the Norwegian explorer, 'conquered' the South Pole in 1911, Shackleton changed his goal: it was now to be the first man to cross the Antarctic Continent on foot.

The *Endurance* sailed from London on 1 August 1914, having secured the Admiralty's command to 'proceed' in spite of the outbreak of war. On board were twenty-seven crew (chosen from 5,000 who

**_Endurance_ crushed in ice.**

**Gentoo Penguin, Grytviken.**

replied to the advertisement), under the command of the New Zealander, Frank Worsley, and sixty-nine sled dogs. From Buenos Aires they sailed next some 800 miles south-east to South Georgia, and on 5 December 1914 they left South Georgia and headed south.

A few days later, in the uncharted Weddell Sea, they encountered their first ice-bergs, of all shapes, sizes and colours, sculptured by the action of the waves, looking like a flotilla of ice ships. Gradually the pack ice closed round the _Endurance_. They kept searching for 'leads' of open water, and managed to reach about eighty miles from the Antarctic continent. But their progress was impeded by foul and freezing weather, so that the ice thickened and hemmed the ship in. They tried to free her from the ice with picks and shovels, and persevered for forty-eight hours. But it was to no avail. Unable to escape from it, the ship was now drifting with the floe, but in the wrong direction. They were trapped and marooned, helpless, and beyond radio link. There was nothing to be done but to steel themselves for a long, dark, sunless winter on the pack ice and to wait for the spring to come. During the day-time the men played football and hockey on the ice, exercised and trained the dogs, and hunted for seals and penguins. In the evenings they resorted to amateur theatre, concerts and playing the gramophone. But steadily the situation worsened. The pressure of the ice on the ship increased, until it began to lift her, while her timbers creaked and groaned and quivered. On 27 October, 1915, she sprang a serious leak, and the decks were breaking up. Shackleton gave the order to lower the life-boats, sledges and all possible provisions, and to haul them onto the flat ice a little way away, and then to abandon ship.

The next days were spent setting up 'Ocean Camp' and salvaging from the ship as many stores and as much food and fuel as they could.

Then during the evening of 21 November 'the Boss' (Shackleton) called out 'She's going, boys!' and the whole crew came out to watch. Here is Shackleton's own description:

> *There was our poor ship a mile and a half away struggling in her death-agony. She went down bows first, her stern raised in the air. She then gave one quick dive, and the ice closed over her for ever.*[1]

Throughout this crisis Shackleton never lost his cool or his confidence. At the same time, an inner conflict was going on. Always putting his men first, his goal for the expedition inevitably changed. It was no longer to cross the Antarctic Continent, but to get all his twenty-nine men back to land. His problem now was not ice but morale.

After an abortive attempt to march across the ice to safety, hauling two

**King Penguins at Grytviken, South Georgia.**

**Unmapped peaks of South Georgia Island.**

of the three lifeboats behind them, a second camp was established on the drifting ice. But on 9 April, when the floe split open under the camp, and the channels became navigable, the three boats were manned and launched. For nearly a week the crew in the open boats were exposed to frightful weather, until they were able to effect a landing on a gravelly spit of Elephant Island, the most northerly of the South Shetlands.

Shackleton now consulted with his senior officers as to where they were most likely to find relief. They settled on South Georgia, whose whaling stations were known to be continuously occupied, 800 miles north-east. Shackleton decided to take with him Frank Worsley, Tom Crean and three hardy Irish sailors – McNeish, McCarthy and Vincent. He then put Frank Wild in charge of the remaining twenty-two.

Having given themselves a few days in which to rest and build up their strength, the six set sail on 24 April on the twenty-foot small but strong ship's whaler, the *James Caird*.

Shackleton describes the next sixteen days as a tale of 'supreme strife amid heaving waters'.[2] Living in extremely cramped quarters, they suffered from frost-bite, and were continuously wet and cold. The *James Caird* was steadily shipping water, so that she was in danger of being swamped. At times they were in dire peril from hurricane-force winds and mountainous waves. During their tenth night, Shackleton wrote how they nearly capsized:

**Chinstrap Penguin with two chicks.**

*During the twenty-six years' experience of the ocean in all its moods I had not encountered a wave so gigantic . . . We felt our boat lifted and flung forward like a cork in breaking surf. We were in a seething chaos of tortured water.*[3]

Above all, the six men were driven almost crazy by their raging thirst. But at last land lay before them, and they succeeded against fearful odds to beach the *James Caird* in King Haakon Bay, South Georgia.

But the whaling station at Grytviken was on the other side of the island: their troubles were far from over. Since neither the boat nor the crew was in a fit state to circumnavigate the island, the only alternative was to walk over its mountainous mass. But nobody had ever penetrated

**Elephant Seal, Grytviken.**

**Shackleton's gravestone, South Georgia.**

more than a mile from its coastline, regarding the interior as inaccessible. Nor had it ever been mapped. Yet there was no other option, and Shackleton never forgot those twenty-two men on Elephant Island, who were waiting to be rescued.

So on 19 May, having allowed themselves a week in which to recover from their arduous sea passage, Ernest Shackleton, Frank Worsley and Tom Crean set out in full moon to cross the island. Ahead of them lay the most formidable and treacherous terrain imaginable. For thirty-six hours, with only short pauses in which to eat and rest, they plodded on − over ridges, across crevasses (for which they were roped), ascending and descending steep snow slopes, cutting steps in the ice, negotiating sheer precipices, and making the final leap to the shore down an icy waterfall.

With long beards, matted hair and tattered garments worn for nearly a year without change, it is hardly surprising that they were not at first recognized by the whalers. Then a night or two of luxurious sleeping and eating were enough for Shackleton, for his mind was preoccupied with the rescue of his marooned men. But his first three attempts failed. First, the large whaler *Southern Sky* set sail for Elephant Island, but when still seventy miles away found her way blocked by an impenetrable barrier of ice. Secondly a Uruguayan trawler steamed steadily south until she too was forced by ice to turn back. Next the chartered schooner *Emma* was similarly forced to turn back. It was the fourth attempt, in the

97

**Near Point Wild, Elephant Island.**

small steamer the *Yelcho*, which had been loaned by the Chilean government, which eventually found the ice open and was able to reach Elephant Island. It was 30 August, and the rescue team received an ecstatic welcome.

Meanwhile, Frank Wild had managed to maintain the morale of his men for four and a half months. Under his supervision the two remaining lifeboats had been upturned and used with other improvised materials to create a hut in which they could live and sleep. Here too they found shelter from the appalling weather (wind, snow, rain and sleet). He carefully rationed their food, so that it would last several months. Cooking and lighting were by oil derived from seal blubber. The cook did his best to vary their diet. A stew of seal bones, limpets and seaweed was popular, and 'breast of penguin' a particular delicacy.

Visiting that spit of land myself in 1991, I wondered if its Chinstrap Penguin rookery included some descendants of those which helped Wild and his men to survive seventy-five years previously. I also marvelled how they could have endured those months in that exposed and restricted spot. Frostbite, cramped quarters, hunger, and the suspense of waiting for rescue all took their toll on the men, and caused days of deep depression. But Shackleton paid Wild this tribute: 'Wild had . . . fought off the devils of despondency and despair on that little sand-spit'. Again, 'his cheery optimism never failed'. One of the men said:

*Wild never gave up hope, and whenever the sea was at all clear of ice, he rolled up his sleeping-bag and said to all hands, 'Roll up your sleeping-bags, boys; the Boss may come today.'*[6]

Shackleton and his men all returned to Britain safely. But they found that the war was still raging. Indeed, it is tragic that, though all survived the rigours of the Antarctic, a number were killed or wounded in action.

As for Shackleton himself, he returned to South Georgia in January 1922, but on the eve of his ship's arrival he suffered a heart attack and died, aged forty-seven. With Lady Shackleton's approval, he was buried in the Grytviken cemetery, where we 'drank his health' in 1991.

His outstanding quality as a leader was undoubtedly his ability to endure hardship. The Shackleton family motto was *Fortitudine Vincimus*, 'by endurance we conquer', and it was surely deliberate that he named his ship *Endurance*. Frank Wild's tribute referred to 'his hardihood and extraordinary powers of endurance, his buoyant optimism when things seemed hopeless, and his unflinching courage in the face of danger'.[7] And the secret of his endurance was surely his Christian faith, however little he expressed it in his journal. These are his words:

*When I look back at those days, I have no doubt that Providence guided us, not only across those snowfields, but across the storm-white sea that separated Elephant Island from our landing-place on South Georgia. I know that during that long and racking march of thirty-six hours over the unnamed mountains and glaciers of South Georgia it seemed to me often that we were four, not three. I said nothing to my companions on the point, but afterwards Worsley said to me. 'Boss, I had a curious feeling on the march that there was another person with us'. Crean confessed to the same idea.*[8]

Penguins surround a bust of Captain Luis Pardo, skipper of MV *Yelcho*, the Chilean vessel which rescued Wild's men.

FOOTNOTES

1. Ernest Shackleton, *South: the story of Shackleton's last expedition 1914-1917* (1919; new ed. Heinemann, 1983), p. 98. See also Caroline Alexander, *The Endurance: Shackleton's legendary Antarctic Expedition* (Knopf, 1998).

2. *South*, p. 165.

3. *South*, pp. 174-5.

4. *South*, p. 219.

5. *South*, p. 237.

6. *South*, p. 220.

7. Frank Wild, *Shackleton's Last Voyage: the story of the Quest* (Cassell, 1923), p. 68.

8. *South*, p. 209.

# 12. Allen Gardiner
## *South American Missionary*

IT WAS IN 1991, TO CELEBRATE MY 70TH BIRTHDAY, that I visited the Falkland Islands (*las islas malvinas* to the Argentinians). Canon Gerry Murphy, Dean of Christ Church Cathedral in Stanley, had invited me to assist him with the Christmas services and to lead a mini-mission there in the New Year. In return, he kindly arranged for me to visit a number of the outlying islands. Keppel Island, off the north shore of West Falkland, held a particular fascination for me, and that for two reasons.

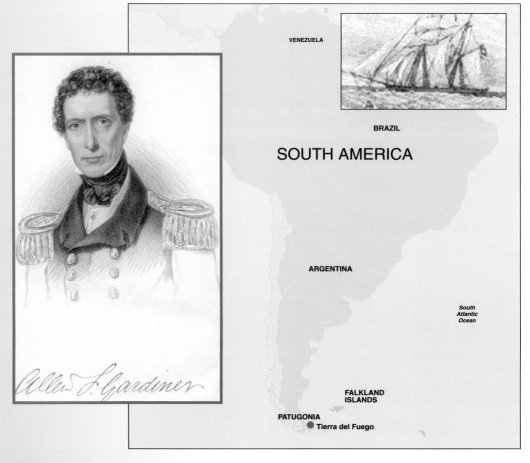

VENEZUELA

BRAZIL

SOUTH AMERICA

ARGENTINA

South
Atlantic
Ocean

FALKLAND
ISLANDS

PATUGONIA
Tierra del Fuego

**Wooden chapel, Keppel Island.**

**Keppel Mission Church, now a barn.**

First, it was the site of two substantial seabird colonies – Black-browed Albatrosses (sitting precariously on their cup-shaped mud nests) and Rockhopper Penguins (with red bill and eyes, and dashing golden eyebrows).

But the even stronger reason for wanting to visit Keppel was its association with that indomitable seafaring missionary, Allen Gardiner, founder of the South American Missionary Society. He chose the Falkland Islands for his mission base, from which to reach the aboriginal tribes of Patagonia and Tierra del Fuego, and after his death it was established on Keppel Island. Today only two or three of the old mission buildings have survived. The wooden chapel, which was dedicated to the English reformers Thomas Cranmer (the Archbishop) and Hugh Latimer (the popular preacher), is now used as a shed for shearing sheep, although the symbol of the South American Missionary Society can still be seen over the door.

Allen Gardiner was born into a Christian upper-class home in Berkshire in the year 1794. From childhood he loved adventure stories, felt the lure of the sea, and resolved to join the Royal Navy – which he did at the age of fourteen. Although he was disappointed not to see active service during the Napoleonic wars (he was only eleven at the time of the Battle of Waterloo), he sailed in both the North Atlantic and the South Atlantic, round Cape Horn and across

101

**Keppel Island, with a colony of Black-browed Albatrosses on the right.**

the Pacific. He also visited Peru and Chile, and saw for himself the sufferings of the neglected Indian tribespeople.

Although Allen Gardiner's parents were practising Christians, he does not seem to have had a living faith himself, until his mother's death and a period of illness turned his thoughts to God. 'After years of ingratitude, unbelief, blasphemy and rebellion', he wrote in his diary, 'have I at last been melted? Alas, how slow, how reluctant I have been to admit the heavenly guest who stood knocking without!'[1]

In 1834 after eleven years of happy married life his wife Julia, who had borne him five children, died. Kneeling by her deathbed, and with her permission, he dedicated the rest of his life to pioneer missionary service.

There now began in his life what Professor Andrew Walls has called 'extraordinary voyages of missionary reconnaissance'.[2] These took him first to South Africa, where he boldly asked the notorious Zulu King Dingane for permission to plant a mission there. Next he sailed to Rio de Janeiro, Montevideo and Buenos Aires, and then led a cavalcade on mule back with his family nearly 1,000 miles across the Andes into Chile, in order to survey the aboriginal scene and assess the opportunities for a mission. Nor must we forget his voyage to Australia, New Guinea and the Dutch East Indies.

Year by year Allen Gardiner's sense of call to the aboriginal tribes of South America deepened. So between 1840 and 1850 he organized no fewer than six expeditions to different parts of the continent, especially to Patagonia and Tierra del Fuego. But consistently his path was blocked, either by the Roman Catholic hierarchy, or by unfriendly and even hostile tribespeople, or by appalling weather conditions in the South Atlantic. Each time he was obliged to withdraw.

After each failed mission Allen Gardiner returned to England to report to his increasingly disappointed supporters and to plan for the next expedition. During this period, because the older missionary societies were unwilling or unable to help, he founded the Patagonia Mission. Its committee kept wavering as to whether it was wise to persevere. Allen Gardiner, however, did not share their hesitations. Whatever they decided, he said,

> *I have made up my mind to go back again to South America, and leave no stone unturned, no effort untried, to establish a mission among the aboriginal tribes. They have a right to be instructed in the gospel of Christ. While God gives me strength, failure shall not daunt me!* [3]

Lesser men would have given up. But Allen Gardiner had put his hand to the plough and refused to turn back. As John Marsh put it, 'with a frame of iron, and nerves which never flinched from fatigue or danger, he broke with dauntless vehemence through every diffi-

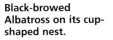

**Black-browed Albatross on its cup-shaped nest.**

**Page from Allen Gardiner's journal.**

*Thursday – There is now no room to doubt that my dear fellow Labourer has ceased from his earthly toils & joined the company of the redeemed in the presence of the Lord whom he served so faithfully – Under these circumstances it was a merciful providence that he left the boat as I could not have removed the body – He left a little peppermint water which he had mixed, & it has been a great comfort to me, but there was no other to drink – Fearing that I might suffer from thirst, I prayed that the Lord would strengthen me to procure some – He graciously answered my petition & yesterday I was enabled to get out & scoop up a sufficient supply from some that trickled down at the stern of the boat by means of one of my indian rubber over shoes – What continued mercies am I receiving at the hands of my heavenly Father! Blessed be his holy name –*

*Friday – Great & marvellous are the loving kindnesses of my gracious God unto me – He has preserved me ... of for 4 days, although without bodily food, without any feeling of hunger or thirst –*

culty which beset his path.'[4] And again, 'if he found it difficult to urge us (*sc.* the committee) forward, we found it impossible to keep him back. Nothing could stop him.'[5]

So preparations went on for his sixth expedition, which turned out to be his last. He selected six men to accompany him – Richard Williams (a doctor), Joseph Erwin (a ship's carpenter), John Maidment (a waiter) and three Cornish fishermen (John Badcock, John Bryant and John Pearce). He also assembled sufficient food supplies to feed seven men for six months.

They reached Spaniard's Harbour on Tierra del Fuego on 5 December 1850. Tierra del Fuego is an archipelago at the southern extremity of the continent, separated from the mainland by the Magellan Strait. No sooner had they arrived there, however, than misfortune after misfortune struck them. First, one of their two launches was irreparably damaged in a storm. Next they lost both landing vessels; their gunpowder (for duck shooting) had been left behind by mistake; and their fishing net had to be abandoned. Then after three

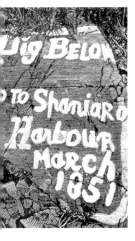

Gardiner's directions to the search party, painted on the rocks. The message reads: 'Dig below. Go to Spaniard Harbour. March 1851.'

*Top:* Artist's romanticised impression of Allen Gardiner's death.

months one of them fell ill with scurvy. Finally, owing to a muddle over the dispatch of a further supply of food, the marooned party looked daily for a relief vessel which never came. One by one they succumbed to a combination of Antarctic weather, disease, exposure and starvation, and died. Allen Gardiner himself was the last to perish. It was the 6 September 1851, nine months after they had reached Tierra del Fuego.

Six weeks later their bodies were found. And not their bodies only, but their diaries too. It is amazing that, wet, cold and hungry, Allen Gardiner should have continued to write his journal until a day or two before he died. It is also astonishing that it survived several weeks of exposure to the elements. 'Blessed be my heavenly Shepherd', he wrote a week before his death, 'he is with me, and I shall not want . . .'.

But the death of the whole group seemed an unmitigated disaster. Years of devoted toil had yielded nothing. No single person had become a disciple of Jesus Christ. No single mission had been established on South American soil. Yet these were not the thoughts which occupied Allen Gardiner's mind while patiently awaiting death. He was not thinking of himself at all, but rather of the aboriginal tribespeople to whom he had dedicated most of his adult life. Even while dying, he was dreaming.

Marooned on the lonely beach he left a wish: 'If I have a wish for the good of my fellow-men, it is that the *Tierra del Fuego mission might*

be prosecuted with vigour . . .'[6]. He also drew up a plan: *'to convey a few of the natives to the Falklands, to teach them English, and learn their language, and to provide a ... schooner of a hundred tons' burden as a mission vessel.'*[7] Then he expressed both his wish and his plan in a prayer:

*Let not this mission fail, though we should not be permitted to labour in it, but graciously raise up other labourers.*[8]

Moreover, considering the scope of the Mission which Allen Gardiner envisaged, comprising not only tribespeople but also 'their neighbours of Spanish descent', it would be advisable, he wrote, to alter the Mission's present designation 'to one more comprehensive and applicable, *viz.* "The South American Missionary Society"'.[9]

The dream, the wish, the plan and the prayer were all fulfilled. The news of the heroic death by starvation of Allen Gardiner and all his men created a sensation in Britain's national press, and it galvanized the church into action. In 1854 a schooner named *Allen Gardiner* sailed to the Falklands, with his only son on board. In 1855 Keppel Island was chosen as the headquarters of the Mission. From then onwards it has never looked back.

In the year 2001 (the 150th anniversary of Allen Gardiner's death) the Anglican Province of the Southern Cone consisted of seven dioceses – Argentina, Northern Argentina, Bolivia, Chile, Paraguay, Peru and Uruguay, and an increasing number of church leaders are Amerindian people. Maurice Sinclair, former Presiding Bishop, is surely right to have summed up the story of SAMS as 'Lonely Death to Overflowing Life'.[10] Yet there remains much more to be done. The stated aim of SAMS is 'to make known the gospel of our Lord Jesus Christ among the Indian tribes and other inhabitants of South America'.

So when I stood on Keppel Island in 1991 I had much to think about. I was of course entranced by the albatrosses and the penguins, but above all I thanked God for the faith and fortitude of Allen Francis Gardiner. And I remembered the sobering words of Jesus: 'unless a kernel of wheat falls to the ground and dies, it remains alone; but if it dies, it multiplies' (John 12:24).

FOOTNOTES

1. Wendy Mann and Henry Sutton, *An Unquenched Flame: a short history of the South American Missionary Society* (SAMS, 1968), p. 23. The diary extract is dated 'September 1822' and is recorded by John W. Marsh and W. H. Stirling in *The Story of Commander Allen Gardiner R.N.* (Nisbet, 1875, 5th edition), p. 4.

2. See his article 'Allen Francis Gardiner' in *Biographical Dictionary of Christian Missions* ed. Gerald H. Anderson (Eerdmans, 1998).

3. John W. Marsh. *op. cit.*, p.31. See also Phyllis Thompson, *An Unquenchable Flame* (Hodder and SAMS, 1983), p. 102.

4. Marsh, *op. cit.*, p. 46, and see Phyllis Thompson, *op. cit.*, p. 129.

5. Phyllis Thompson, *op. cit.*, p. 128.

6. John W. Marsh *op. cit.*, p. 78.

7. John W. Marsh, *op. cit.*, pp. 78–79.

8. Phyllis Thompson, *op. cit.*, p. 179.

9. Phyllis Thompson, *op. cit.*, p.188.

10. From an article by Maurice Sinclair in *SHARE* magazine, January–March 2002.

# 13. Charles Darwin

## *Visiting the Galapagos*

*Let no man . . . think or maintain that a man can search too far or be too well studied in the book of God's Word or in the book of God's Works, divinity or philosophy; but rather let men endeavour an endless progress or proficiency in both.*

THESE WORDS COME FROM THE PEN OF FRANCIS BACON, the seventeenth century English philosopher and statesman. They conclude his book *The Advancement of Learning* (1605). But Charles Darwin found them there and put them on the flyleaf of his book *The Origin of Species* (1859).

It is an intriguing concept that God has written not one book, but two. The book of God's Word we call 'Scripture', and the book of God's Works 'Nature'. Both are divine revelations, the disclosure of God's glory in nature and of his grace in Scripture. Moreover, he invites us to

**VENEZUELA**

**EQUADOR**

**GALAPAGOS ISLANDS**

*South Pacific Ocean*

**SOUTH AMERICA**

**Sunset over Daphne and Santiago islands.**

study both, so that nature study and Bible study should go hand in hand. And as we engage in these studies, we find ourselves, in the famous words of the German astronomer Johannes Kepler, 'thinking God's thoughts after him'.

In consequence, there is an important correspondence between theology and science. Theology is the human attempt to understand and synthesize what God has revealed in Scripture, while science is the human attempt to understand and systematize what God has revealed in nature.

There should, therefore, be no conflict between the two, since all truth is God's truth, whether it is biblical or scientific. Indeed, the creation – evolution debate, especially when it involved a headlong confrontation, has been largely unnecessary, and remains confused and confusing today. The reason for this is that it has been, and still is, conducted in 'conditions of low visibility'. That is to say, the participants have tended to plunge into combat without first pausing to define their terms. When people affirm that creation and evolution are incompatible with each other, what do they mean by 'creation'? And what do they mean by 'evolution'?

First, it must not be assumed that 'creation' can only mean a literal, six-day programme. That understanding of creation is certainly incom-

A Marine Iguana, with a sharp dorsal comb.

patible with evolution, if only because each has a totally different time-span. No. All Christians believe in creation, including those who do not subscribe to young earth creationism. One might even go so far as to say that one cannot be a Christian and not believe in creation. The apostles' creed, which is the universal faith of the church, begins with the dogmatic assertion 'I believe in God, the Father Almighty, Creator of heaven and earth'.

Secondly, it must not be supposed that 'evolution' can only mean a blind and purely random process in which God has been eliminated from his universe and replaced by 'Chance'. This understanding of evolution is indeed incompatible with creation, inasmuch as chance and purpose exclude one another. Those Christians who believe in evolution, however, mean that the huge variety of animal and vegetable forms can best be accounted for not by the independent creation of each, but by a gradual process of 'descent with modification', whether or not Darwin's 'natural selection' is the best explanation of its mechanism.

The fact is that the theory of evolution remains but a working hypothesis. It continues to be criticized by both scientists and philosophers, now for 'its lack of philosophical stringency' (meaning 'everything to everyone'), now 'because it is not falsifiable', and now 'because it has no predictive value'.[1]

There are also many Christians who consider that any form of evolution contradicts, or is contradicted by, the early chapters of Genesis. We would be wise to remember, however, that the Bible is essentially a book of salvation, not of science. It has been given to us in order to unfold the way of salvation through Christ, which we could not know otherwise, and not to reveal scientific truths which human beings could themselves discover by the empirical method. I do not mean by this that the biblical and the scientific accounts of things are necessarily incompatible, but rather that they are complementary. Their purposes are different. Science addresses itself to 'how' things function; Scripture is preoccupied with 'why' questions.

A Land Iguana – 'few animals are uglier'.

What, then, does Genesis 1 teach about origins? Six lessons stand out: (1) that God created everything out of an original nothing; (2) that his creation proceeded in progressive stages; (3) that the means of his creation was his will (Rev. 4:11), expressed in his Word; (4) that man, male and female, bearing God's image, is the crown of creation; (5) that everything God made was good, and (6) that what he created he continues to sustain.

**Sixto, navigator and cook for the author's trip to the Galapagos.**

Darwin himself does not seem to have renounced his belief in creation when he developed his belief in evolution. In this respect I am glad to have read his *Autobiography*, consisting of recollections and letters compiled and edited by his son Francis. In it he expresses 'the impossibility of conceiving that this grand and wondrous universe, with our conscious selves, arose through chance, seems to me the chief argument for the existence of God'. He also considered 'that the theory of evolution is quite compatible with the belief in a God'.[2] At the same time he confesses to fluctuations in his faith.[3] It is obvious that throughout his life he was caught in a dilemma between belief and unbelief. Colin Russell quotes him:

> I am conscious that I am in an utterly hopeless muddle. I cannot think that the world, as we see it, is the result of chance; and yet I cannot look at each separate thing as the result of design.[4]

**Blue-footed Booby with chick and egg, Daphne Island.**

Charles Darwin was born in 1809, went up to Edinburgh as a medical student, and transferred to Cambridge to train for the pastoral ministry of the Church of England. But he spent much of his time hunting and shooting, and collecting plants and beetles. Graduating in 1831, aged twenty-two, he was invited by Captain Robert FitzRoy to sail round the world with him on HMS *Beagle* as the ship's naturalist. In

**Medium Ground Finch, one of the 13 species of Finch which Darwin identified.**

the end the voyage lasted five years, and changed his life.

His most memorable stop was the month he spent on and around the Galapagos, the archipelago of volcanic islands some 600 miles off the west coast of Ecuador. I read his account of this visit[5] with the greatest interest, for in 1977 my Argentinian friend Dr René Padilla and I spent a week visiting some of the very islands he visited.

The islands are widely dispersed, and the archipelago measures more than 100 miles north to south and east to west. So we chartered a five-ton, sea-worthy boat called *Cristo Rey* ('Christ the King'), skippered by José, with Sixto serving as both navigator and cook.

We dropped anchor in a beautiful green-water lagoon of Santa Fe island on whose beaches about fifty sea lions (in Spanish *lobos marinos* or 'sea wolves') were basking. But the noise they made resembled neither a wolf's bark, nor a lion's roar. They can moo like a cow, bleat like a sheep, bray like a donkey, and even belch with conspicuous vulgarity like a drunkard. The colony showed no sign of fear. Indeed, they were mostly asleep. They allowed us to walk round and through them. We then had fish for supper, caught and cooked by Sixto, while Brown Pelicans fished in the lagoon and the sea lions kept up their intermittent chorus.

Our next destination was Española or Hood island, the most south-easterly of the archipelago. The cliff ledges were occupied by Masked Boobies (Gannets), dazzling white except for black edges to their wings and tail and their black facial mask. Further inland we came to a colony of Waved Albatrosses. Española is their only breeding ground in the world, and there are said to be 12,000 pairs on the island. A dozen or so pairs, with newly hatched chicks were very accessible. They sat majestic and defiant, concealing their 7-8 feet wing span, watching us with their big, black, beady eyes, and clacking their huge yellow bill sharply if they felt any alarm.

On several islands we became acquainted with the two species of iguana which are confined to the Galapagos. The marine iguana is black with red back markings. It inhabits rocky sea beaches, and walks on the sea bed feeding on seaweed and algae. The land iguana, however, is yellowish-orange beneath and brownish-red above, with a livid yellow head and front feet. It lives in burrows, is also a herbivore, specializing in cactus plants. Both iguanas grow up to three feet in length and look like primitive dragons with sharp dorsal combs. Darwin called them 'hideous-looking creatures', while Captain FitzRoy went further and

**The author astride a giant tortoise, Galapagos Islands.**

declared that 'few animals are uglier'. But I find this a rather harsh judgment. Grotesque, perhaps, and even fearsome, but very docile, and skilled in clambering over the rocks.

On Santa Cruz island a primary schoolboy called Mario was appointed our guide in looking for giant tortoises ('*galapagos*') which gave the archipelago its name. We found two, one of which Mario said was about 150 years old, as he leaped gleefully onto its back. Some of these tortoises, Darwin wrote, grow to immense proportions, weigh up to 500 pounds, and require six to eight men to lift them. 'I frequently got on their backs', Darwin continued, 'and then, giving a few raps on the hinder part of their shells, they would rise up and walk away, but I found it very difficult to keep my balance'.[6] In Mario's case, as he sat astraddle the enormous tortoise, grinning from ear to ear, it sagged, withdrew into its carapace, and issued a hissing sound as when a rubber mattress is deflated.

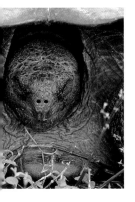

**Tortoise head. 'Such worshipful venerableness of aspect.'**

'These huge reptiles', Darwin wrote, 'seemed to my fancy like some antediluvian animals'. Herman Melville, author of *Moby Dick*, was more eloquent in his comments; 'they seemed newly crawled forth from beneath the foundations of the world . . . Such worshipful venerableness of aspect!' Darwin was fascinated by the variations between them. Each island seemed to have its own endemic subspecies, and they differed from one another in the pattern of their carapace, in some physical features, and in their feeding habits.

**Dr René Padilla of Argentina face to face with a Waved Albatross.**

**A Great Blue Heron bade us a rather haughty farewell.**

Darwin observed a similar diversity in the finches. 'A most singular group of finches', he called them, 'related to each other in the structure of their beaks, short tails, form of body and plumage'.[7] 'Darwin's Finches' they are now called, and there are thirteen species of them.

So the Galapagos is a living laboratory of mini-evolution. It is appropriate that a Darwin Research Station was established there in 1964, and that it had been declared a National Park five years earlier

Yet the whole area is extremely vulnerable. For centuries the islands had been devastated by looting sailors. Next domestic animals (dogs, goats and pigs) were introduced, became wild, and are doing much damage. Then in 2000 local fishermen, whose lobster quota was reduced, staged a violent protest; and in 2001 a tanker spilled 200,000 gallons of oil. Meanwhile the tourist trade continues to grow and to threaten the endemic wildlife and its habitat. Every possible effort needs to be taken to protect this unique archipelago.

FOOTNOTES

1. Wilma George, *Darwin*, Fontana Modern Masters series (1982), p. 139.

2. *Autobiography of Charles Darwin*, with two appendices, by his son Sir Francis Darwin (Watts, 1929), p. 142.

3. *Ibid.*, p. 149.

4. Colin A. Russell, *Cross-currents: interactions between science and faith* (IVP, 1985), p. 154.

5. Charles Darwin, *The Voyage of the Beagle* (John Murray, 1897), chapter xvii, pp. 357-385.

6. *Voyage*, p. 369.

7. *Voyage*, p. 363.

# 14. D. L. Moody
## *The American student world*

*On February 5, 1837, there was born of poor parents in a humble farmhouse in Northfield, Massachusetts, a little baby who was to become the greatest man as I believe, of his generation or his century – Dwight L. Moody. After our great generals, great statesmen, great scientists and great men of letters have passed away and been forgotten, and their work and its helpful influence has come to an end, the work of D. L. Moody will go on and its saving influence continue and increase, bringing blessing not only to every state in the Union but to every nation on earth.[1]*

THUS WROTE REUBEN ARCHER TORREY, who became Moody's disciple, associate and successor. His tribute to Moody sounds fulsome, but he was as close to Moody as anybody, and he certainly believed what he wrote.

It goes without saying that I never met D. L. Moody, for he was born in 1837 and died in 1899. Yet I feel as if I knew him. As a young man and new convert I was given a copy of R. A. Torrey's striking little book *Why God Used D. L. Moody* (1923), and I was inspired by it.

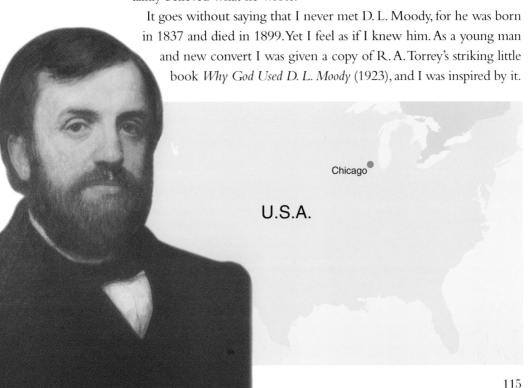

Chicago

U.S.A.

Since then I have read the official biography *The Life of Dwight L. Moody* (1900) by his son William, and John C. Pollock's fascinating account *Moody without Sankey* (1963). I am also familiar with the two most recent biographies – *Love Them In* by Stanley N. Gundry (1976/1999) and A *Passion for Souls* by Lyle W. Dorsett (1997). In addition, I have preached in Moody Memorial Church, Chicago; lectured at Moody Bible Institute; been interviewed on WMBI (Moody's popular radio programme); read books published by Moody Press; and viewed Fact and Faith films produced by Moody Institute of Science. Perhaps these second-hand proximities give me at least a minimum warrant to introduce him to you.

What Billy Graham was to the twentieth century Dwight Moody was to the nineteenth. There are remarkable similarities between them, even though they were separated by a century. Both were US citizens, mass evangelists and gifted communicators. Both attracted a huge following, from all strata of society and on both sides of the Atlantic. Both believed and preached the biblical gospel. Both were men of personal integrity, whose authenticity shone brightly and was everywhere recognized. Both were concerned for the social implications of the gospel, and specially for racial reconciliation. Both strove for Christian unity on the basis of the gospel. Both were sincere, humble, gracious and generous. Above all, the hand of the Lord was on them both.

Another interesting parallel between Billy Graham and D. L. Moody is that they both loved students and both preached the good news of Christ to the Universities of Oxford and Cambridge.

Moody's Cambridge University mission in 1882 was specially memorable. Although his recent mission in London had been signally blessed, friends and critics alike wondered

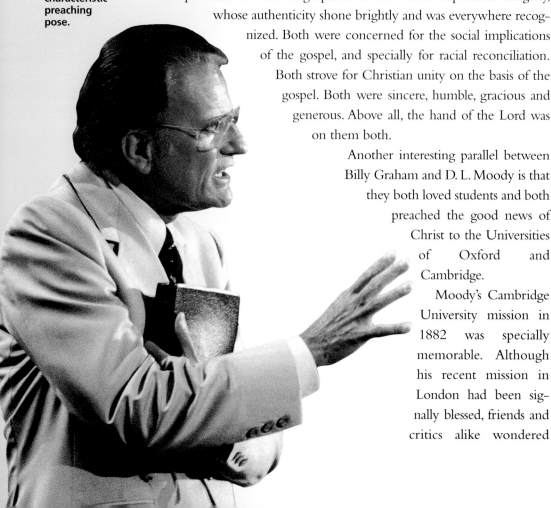

The evangelist Billy Graham in a characteristic preaching pose.

*Right:* **D. L. Moody preaching at the Agricultural Hall, Islington, London.**

how he would go down in a seat of learning like Cambridge. It was known that he was not himself a university graduate. Moreover, his preaching style was simple, even simplistic, and some would say coarse. Moody himself confessed to feeling nervous.

The mission was scheduled to open on 5 November. This was a foolish choice of date because in Britain 5 November is Guy Fawkes Day, the anniversary of the discovery of the Gunpowder Plot (the unsuccessful conspiracy to blow up the Houses of Parliament in 1605), which is celebrated with fireworks and bonfires. A boisterous crowd of nearly 2000 men assembled, pushing and shoving, joking and laughing, determined on some good fun at the American visitor's expense.

**The Gatehouse, King's College, Cambridge.**

The entry of the platform party was greeted with applause, the opening prayer with 'Hear! Hear!' instead of 'Amen', a Sankey hymn with 'Encore', and other parts of the meeting with cries of 'Well done!' A firecracker was thrown against a window and exploded on impact. Cheers and jeers continued throughout, even after the police had been obliged to evict the worst rowdies. But all the time Moody soldiered on, refusing to lose his cool.[2]

On the following evenings the crowd was smaller and more disciplined. People had been stung by an article in the *Cambridge Review*, which complained of the ungentlemanly behaviour of Sunday night. One undergraduate came to Moody to apologize. Several made public professions of faith. Then on the final Sunday the hall was packed, the audience listened attentively, and many responded to the gospel.

The main door into
Moody Bible
Institute, downtown
Chicago.

The main door into Moody Bible Institute, downtown Chicago.

Looking back, J. H. Moulton, then an undergraduate, later a distin-guished New Testament scholar, said: 'I regard that week as the most momentous week in the religious history of this country during my lifetime . . . '.[3]

It was long before the Cambridge University mission, however, that Moody became involved in the student world, and specially in the YMCA, which had spread throughout the USA and included in its membership a high percentage of students.

In 1886, at the instigation of some YMCA leaders, D. L. Moody wel-comed 250 students to a month-long Bible conference at his Mount Hermon campus in Northfield, Massachusetts. Under the influence of Robert Wilder, a senior from Princeton, the topic of mission came to dominate the conference, and by the end of the month 100 students had committed themselves to become foreign missionaries.

Then in 1888, at a similar conference, the Student Volunteer Movement for Foreign Missions (SVM) came into being, with John R. Mott as its chairman and Robert Wilder as its travelling secretary. They adopted the watchword 'The Evangelization of the World in this gen-

*Overall*: Contemporary drawing of D. L. Moody.

*Bottom*: D. L. Moody with neighbourhood children from his Sunday School class.

eration', intending it as a statement of responsibility, not of prophecy. On joining, the volunteer made the following pledge: 'It is my purpose, if God permit, to become a foreign missionary.'[4]

From then on, an international student missionary convention, sponsored by the SVM, was held every four years. David Howard writes:

> For the next twenty-five years, the story of the SVM is one of constant growth and outreach . . . By 1945, at the most conservative estimate, 20,500 students . . . reached the field.

The 1920 Convention marked the peak of the movement's growth, with 6,890 people in attendance. But from this high point the SVM went into rapid decline, and by the beginning of World War II it had lost its vision and its zeal.

Meanwhile, another student movement had come into being in North America, the Inter-Varsity Christian Fellowship, and in 1946 it held in Toronto its first student missionary convention. 575 students attended, and the old flame of the SVM was rekindled. A second student missionary convention was held the following year, culminating on New Year's Day 1948, with the slogan 'From every campus to every country'. 1,294 students attended. From then onwards a triennial student missionary convention has been held at the University of Illinois in Champaign–Urbana. The university auditorium is a circular concrete structure like a huge mushroom, seating 18,000 people. Yet somehow at the 1990 convention more than 19,000 people were in attendance.

I had the privilege of speaking at six Urbana conventions from 1964 to 1979. Every convention has included plenary sessions for worship, instruction and exhortation, and seminars and workshops on a large number of different topics. It concludes on New Year's Eve with a moving Communion service, in which we hear the Word of God, receive the bread and wine, exchange the peace, and sing 'We rest on thee, and in thy name we go' to the tune *Finlandia*. Then as the New Year dawns at midnight, thousands of students leave immediately for their homeward journeys by chartered bus, some heading for distant destinations two or three days away. It is not fanciful to trace much of this contemporary student missionary enthusiasm to D. L. Moody's Bible conference at Northfield in 1886.

As I conclude this brief introduction of D. L. Moody, I return to R. A. Torrey's little book *Why God Used D. L. Moody*. The very first reason Torrey gives is that Moody 'was a fully surrendered man', so that 'every ounce of that two-hundred-and-eighty-pound body of his belonged to God'. Yet, great bear of a man though he was, he also exhibited true humility and gentleness.

Moody's sons remember the times when he lost his temper with them:

*After they had gone to bed, they would hear those heavy footsteps, and he'd come into their room and put a heavy hand on their head and say 'I want you to forgive me; that wasn't the way Christ taught.'*[5]

Somebody else once said of Moody: 'The man of iron will proved that he had mastered the hardest words of all earth's languages, 'I am sorry.'

FOOTNOTES

1. R. A. Torrey, *Why God Used D. L. Moody* (Revell, 1923), p. 5.

2. A full account of the 1882 Moody Mission is given in *A Cambridge Movement* by J. C. Pollock (John Murray, 1953), pp. 57-70; in *Moody Without Sankey* by J. C. Pollock (Hodder & Stoughton, 1963), pp. 200-208. Also in *Whatever Happened to the Jesus Lane Lot?* by Oliver R. Barclay (IVP, 1977), pp. 22-30.

3. *Moody Without Sankey*, p. 207.

4. The story of the SVM is well told by David Howard in *Student Power in World Evangelism* (IVP, 1970).

5. *Moody Without Sankey*, p. 235.

6. *Ibid.*, p. 189.

# 15. John Franklin
## *Seeking the North West Passage*

T HE QUEST FOR THE NORTH WEST PASSAGE, that is, for a sea
route from Labrador in the North Atlantic to Alaska in the
North Pacific, was initially fired by the Elizabethan spirit of
adventure. More particularly, it was motivated by a threefold ambition
– to open up trade with the Far East, to map the unknown regions of
the frozen north, and to bring honour and glory to Britain.

So during the sixteenth and seventeenth centuries notable expeditions were led by Martin Frobisher (1576-1578),
John Davis (1585-1587), Henry Hudson (1610)
and William Baffin (1612-1616), whose surnames
have left an indelible mark on the Arctic, in
Frobisher Bay, Davis Strait, Hudson Bay and Baffin
Island (although understandably now European

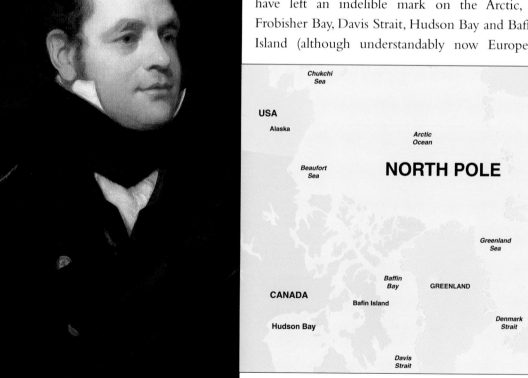

names are being replaced by Inuit words). But those early explorers' fragile vessels, constructed of wood and powered by wind, were not equipped to withstand the pressures of sea ice.

It was not until after the Napoleonic wars that the search for the North West Passage was resumed. It will for ever be associated with the name of John Franklin. Born in 1786, he joined the British navy as a fourteen-year-old cadet, served for three years on HMS *Investigator*, surveying the coastline of Australia under Matthew Flinders, and saw active service in the Battle of Trafalgar in 1805.

During the 1820s several more expeditions were launched, in the quest for the North West Passage. Most of them approached their goal either from the east (the North Atlantic) or from the west (the North Pacific), but Franklin led two overland expeditions from the south (Hudson Bay). He was given the specific task of surveying 500 miles of North American coastline between the mouth of the Mackenzie River and the mouth of the Coppermine River.

It is at this point in the story that I take the liberty of making a personal intrusion. For while John Franklin was surveying the North American coastline, he also mapped the intricacies of Bathurst Inlet. Not far from its south-western corner, at the mouth of the Burnside

**Arctic Lupins.**

River, there lies a cluster of green fibre-glass igloos and other buildings known as 'Bathurst Inlet Lodge'. Originally a Hudson Bay trading post, it was developed in the 1960s and 70s by Glenn and Trish Warner, in collaboration with the local Inuit community, as a lodge for wildlife enthusiasts.

For a few years I served as honorary chaplain to the Inuit colony. So I have every reason to be grateful to Rear-Admiral Sir John Franklin for his skills as a cartographer. It is hard to describe the grandeur of the local scenery. All around is a magnificent panorama of tundra, hills and valleys, rivers, lakes, islands and sea, with the nearest other human habitation about sixty miles away. During the brief Arctic summer, when the surface snow and ice melt, 'God's garden' of wild flowers comes into bloom – Arctic lupins, poppies and saxifrage, mountain dryas and Indian paintbrush. The natural pasture is enjoyed by the population of breeding birds and grazed by caribou and muskoxen.

Franklin's first overland expedition (1819-1822) was an almost total disaster. Faced with the possibility of starvation, he and his men were reduced to the extremity of eating the soft leather of their moccasin shoes, and were rescued only just in time by three Indians. When Franklin went home to England, he was nicknamed 'the man who ate his own boots'! His second overland expedition (1825-1827) was deemed a success.

During this same period other attempts to find the North West Passage were made, especially by Edward Parry in the 1820s, and by James and John Ross in the early 1830s. They astonished the watching world by their ability to endure several winters in a row in Arctic cold and darkness. Each expedition added more pieces to the jigsaw of the Arctic archipelago.

It was in 1845 that Franklin took centre stage, with an official naval expedition which he hoped and believed would complete the discovery of the North West Passage. He captained the *Erebus* and the *Terror*, both of which had just been equipped with auxiliary power in the form of a steam engine (although they had coal for only twelve days). Each ship was amply supplied with food to last three years, a sizeable library, a hand organ, Bibles and prayer books. On Sunday 18 May, Sir John Franklin read Divine Service on board, and the following day 134 officers and men sailed down the River Thames, assured of the good will of the entire nation. They were sighted by a whaling vessel

**Lady Jane Franklin.**

**The first rescue attempt to find Franklin by the *Enterprise* and the *Investigator*.**

in July, but then they vanished off the face of the planet; they were never seen again.

John Franklin had married Jane Griffin in November 1828. She has been described as a 'woman of great vivacity, loyalty, intellect, spirit and charm'.[1] By the end of 1846 she gave voice to her growing apprehension regarding the fate of her husband and his men, and she began a campaign of agitation. She appealed to the Admiralty, the Prime Minister, the President of the United States, and even the Emperor of Russia, urging them to take further initiatives to find the missing ships and their crews. During the next ten years about forty expeditions were launched, both official and unofficial, both British and American. The year 1847 was a period of intense anxiety. And when in 1848 the first rescue vessels returned with no news, everybody more or less gave up hope. But not Jane. Her search went on, if not for survivors, then at least for any relics or records which might throw light on the fate of the *Erebus* and the *Terror* and their personnel.

True to her indomitable character, Jane Franklin wrote a number of letters to her husband, which in due course were returned to her, undelivered and unopened. Here is an extract from one of them.

*I desire nothing but to cherish you the remainder of your days, however injured and broken your health may be – but in every case I will strive to bow to the Almighty Will, and trust through His mercy for a blessed reunion in a better world! . . . I live in you my own dearest – I pray for you at all hours.*

Not until August 1850 were the first clues found on Beechey Island. It is not actually an island but a small peninsula, joined to Devon Island by a narrow isthmus of shingle. Here some pieces of clothing, naval stores and meat tins were found, and nearby three graves with wooden head-stones commemorating John Torrington, John Hartnell and William Braine, who had all died between January and April 1846.

Here I venture to intrude again. Having spent a night at Resolute on Cornwallis Island in June 1986, a group of us flew to Beechey Island in a Twin Otter on skis. We landed below a sheltered ridge and climbed through thick snow up to the monument which had been erected to Franklin and his men, and to those who had died while searching for them. It was surrounded by the rusty remains of bully beef tins and of barrel stays. We then trudged a quarter of a mile or so to the graves, following some fresh polar bear paw prints. One of our party carried the statutory rifle as a precaution. The grave headstones are now fibre glass replicas, the wooden originals being housed in a museum. The most legible of the three reads as follows:

**A giant iceberg near Resolute, which had floated down from Ellesmere Island in the far north.**

*Above*: Grave head-stone of John Torrington.

*Right*: Beechey Island, where Franklin and his men spent the winter of 1845-6. Some graves are seen in the fore-ground.

*Sacred to the memory of*
*John Torrington*
*who departed this life January 1st*
AD *1846*
*on board of H.M. ship* Terror
*aged 20 years*

It was a poignant moment to stand in silence by those eloquent graves and to wonder what had caused the deaths of those young men 140 years previously. We knew that in 1984 Dr Owen Beattie (an anthropologist) and John Geiger (a journalist), together with others representing different disciplines, had obtained permission to exhume the three bodies and conduct an autopsy, in order if possible to discover the cause of their deaths. Their work was finished in June 1986, the same month as our visit. The remarkable photographs of the disinterred bodies reveal that, buried in the permafrost, they had been almost perfectly preserved in that natural refrigerator.

Putting together the various relics and reports which later expeditions gathered, it appears that John Franklin and his men spent the winter of 1845-6 on Beechey Island; that John Franklin himself died there on 11 June 1847; that the ships were hemmed in by thick ice; and that the 105 survivors eventually abandoned ship in April 1848. They began to walk, pulling sledges, towards a Hudson Bay Company's post, but (according to an Inuk's account) they dropped dead as they walked.

A monument was erected in that desolate place to commemorate both Franklin's crew and those who died while searching for them.

The major cause of their death was almost certainly scurvy. It was already well known that the body's necessary anti-scorbutic factor could be supplied by lemon juice, but the statutory naval ration of one ounce a day was not enough. They also relied on salted and tinned meat, instead of learning from the Eskimos (who were free of scurvy) the value of the fresh meat of seal, bear and caribou. So Franklin's men 'dropped in their tracks, their gums blackened, their teeth rattling loosely in their heads, their flesh spongy and sunken from internal bleeding, weakened, debilitated' – the victims of scurvy.[3]

Next, Owen Beattie's autopsy team subjected samples of the men's tissue, hair and bone to laboratory tests, which revealed that they contained much higher than normal levels of lead. And Dr Beattie's own study of the food tins near the graves revealed that the solder used (90 per cent lead) had not completely sealed the tins' seams, thus exposing those eating the contents to serious lead poisoning.

Owen Beattie and John Geiger end their book with this conclusion:

> It is sadly ironic that Franklin's mighty expedition, certainly one of the greatest seafaring expeditions ever launched, carrying all the tools that early industry and innovation could offer, should have been mortally wounded by one of them . . . None could have known that inside the tins stored in the ships' hold there ticked a time bomb that helped not only to deny Franklin his triumph, but to steal away 129 brave lives . . .'[4]

An artist's impression of an early nineteenth century meeting of British naval officers (inappropriately uniformed) with native fur-clad Inuits.

Yet there is more to say. Behind the physical problems (scurvy and lead poisoning) there lay a deeper cultural one which has thwarted much Arctic exploration. The editor of a recent recension of Franklin's journal attributed the failure of his first overland expedition to 'an inability to adapt to the ways of Indians and voyageurs (the Canadian word for northern guides and explorers) who knew the country so well . . .'. Franklin was, in fact, 'a solid representative of imperial culture' in its negative as well as its positive aspects. Today we might describe him as 'ethnocentric'.[5]

On the one hand, he and his brother officers never left behind the symbols of British upper class society. A drawing has survived, which depicts a historic encounter in 1818 between two British naval officers and a group of Greenland Eskimos. The Eskimos are appropriately clad in furs and sealskins, whereas the naval officers are still wearing their gold-braided uniforms, tailcoats, cocked hats, white gloves and buckled shoes, just as if they had dressed for a parade in London.[6] There was to be no lowering of decorum in the Royal Navy! Among the ships' relics were found twenty-six Victorian silver spoons and forks, each bearing the crest or monogram of an officer, together with elegant china and cut glass. So they evidently continued to dine in their accustomed style. But it is 'puzzling that so many heavy and obviously useless items were ever taken ashore',[7] for this unnecessary weight will have seriously impeded the progress of the men who were pulling the sledges overland.

Not only did naval officers not leave behind the trappings of their own culture but, on the other hand, they do not seem to have appreciated Indian or Inuit culture enough to be willing to learn from them valuable lessons in diet, dress and hunting skills. The most successful Arctic explorers were those who 'adopted the Eskimo way of life'.[8] Franklin's men died, wrote a twentieth century Scandinavian explorer, 'because they brought their environment with them; they were not prepared and had not learned how to adapt to another'.[9]

There is surely a lesson to learn here in cultural humility.

FOOTNOTES

1. Ann Savours, *The Search for the Northwest Passage* (Chatham Publishing, 1999), p. 167.

2. Quoted by Ann Savours, *op. cit.*, p. 192.

3. Pierre Berton, *Arctic Grail: the quest for the Northwest Passage and the North Pole 1818-1909* (1988; Lyons Press, 2000), p. 146.

4. Owen Beattie and John Geiger, *Frozen in Time: the fate of the Franklin Expedition* (Bloomsbury, 1987), p. 162.

5. Ann Savours, *op. cit.*, p. 79.

6. Pierre Berton, *op. cit.*, pp. 14, 15.

7. Ann Savours, *op. cit.*, p. 297.

8. *Ibid.*, p. 302.

9. Pierre Berton, *op. cit.*, p. 337.

# 16. Thomas Becket
## *Canterbury and Choughs*

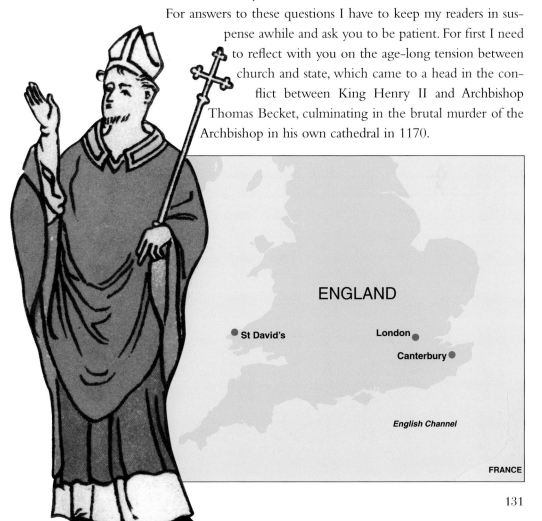

With THOMAS BECKET I COMPLETE MY CIRCULAR JOURNEY round the world in eighty years, for I return to West Wales where my journey began.

But what on earth has a twelfth century Archbishop of Canterbury to do with West Wales? Canterbury in Kent and the west coast of Wales are more than three hundred miles apart, on opposite sides of southern Britain. How can they relate to one another?

For answers to these questions I have to keep my readers in suspense awhile and ask you to be patient. For first I need to reflect with you on the age-long tension between church and state, which came to a head in the conflict between King Henry II and Archbishop Thomas Becket, culminating in the brutal murder of the Archbishop in his own cathedral in 1170.

ENGLAND

St David's

London

Canterbury

English Channel

FRANCE

**The cloisters, Canterbury Cathedral.**

Any reflection on church and state will profitably begin with the enigmatic epigram of Jesus:

*Render to Caesar the things that are Caesar's, and to God the things that are God's (Mark 12:17).*

Though somewhat cryptic, this saying clearly implies that some things belong to Caesar and other things to God; that God's people are to discern which is which; and that they must not confuse them. Further, church history has witnessed a struggle between the two. When the state has tried to control the church, we have since the sixteenth century called it 'Erastianism'. 'Theocracy' connotes the opposite extreme when the church has tried to control the state. And between these two extremes there have been various attempts at compromise in fulfilment of Jesus' epigram.

So now let me remind you of the story of Thomas Becket and of his fifty-two stormy years.

He was born in London in 1118 of well-to-do Norman parents, who had come to settle in England. He was educated in London and Paris, and then studied law in Italy. During these formative years he showed clear signs of great intelligence.

In his twenties Thomas was introduced to Theobald, Archbishop of Canterbury, who recognized his talents, took him into his household, ordained him deacon, sent him on several diplomatic missions, and in

1154 appointed him to the senior administrative post of Archdeacon of Canterbury.

The same year (1154) Henry of Anjou acceded to the British throne as King Henry II. He was only twenty-one years old, fifteen years younger than Thomas Becket, but they became intimate friends, Thomas serving as Henry's constant companion and counsellor.

The following year (1155), on Theobald's recommendation, Henry appointed Thomas his Chancellor. He assumed this heavy responsibility with conspicuous ability. As one historian has written:

**Canterbury Cathedral, Kent, England.**

> *his personal efficiency, lavish entertainment and support for the king's interests even, on occasion, against those of the church, made him a quite outstanding royal official.*[1]

It looked as if he had a brilliant political career ahead of him.

But in 1161 Archbishop Theobald died, and in his place Henry was resolved to secure the election of his friend and chancellor, Thomas. Henry believed that Thomas's close and supportive friendship would continue in his new role, and even increase, and that Thomas would not resist the king's tendency to interfere in the church's business. But Thomas anticipated this future conflict of interests, and is said to have confronted the king with it:

> *Should God permit me to be Archbishop of Canterbury, I should lose your Majesty's favour, and the affection with which you honour me would be changed into hatred. For several things you do in prejudice to the rights of the church make me fear that you would require of me what I could not agree to; and envious persons would not fail to make this the occasion of endless strife between us.*[2]

Thomas was right. His foresight was accurate. What he feared happened. The situation in which Thomas found himself as simultaneously Chancellor and Archbishop is the stuff which high drama is made of. Thomas believed that the conflict of loyalties would be intolerable. So, no sooner had he become Archbishop than he resigned as Chancellor. He also adopted an austere lifestyle in order to express his change of role. It is understandable that Henry was deeply disappointed. Indeed, the seeds of future conflict between the two men, who had been such close friends, were sown at this time. Their relationship rapidly worsened. At base the issue was simple. The King was determined to curb the privileges of the church, and the Archbishop was determined to

**Choughs on Becket's escutcheon (coat of arms).**

curb the interference of the King. For example, the king resolved to abolish 'benefit of clergy', namely that clerics convicted in a church court were exempt from sentencing and punishment by a secular court.

Then the so-called 'Constitutions of Clarendon' covered a wider field. They codified the customs which the King had inherited from his grandfather Henry I. By these Henry II wanted to define relations between church and state, to control and reduce appeals to Rome, to regulate excommunication, and to recognize the Pope's jurisdiction only in a formal way. At first, though reluctantly, Thomas was inclined to acquiesce in these regulations, but the Pope refused to approve them and, when he saw their implications, Thomas rejected them too. Henry and Thomas were now in serious confrontation, and Thomas fled to France.

**The murder of Thomas Becket in Canterbury Cathedral, from a fourteenth century miniature.**

Choughs' nesting cave, Deer Park, near Marloes, Pembrokeshire.

For six years (1164-70) Thomas remained in exile. During this time he engaged in some negotiations between King, Archbishop and Pope, but none of them was willing to give way.

In the end a nominal reconciliation permitted Thomas to return to Canterbury (to a rapturous popular welcome), but it was shallow and short-lived. In a fit of ungovernable rage Henry rashly asked who would rid him of 'this turbulent priest'. Four knights heard his words, interpreted them literally, rode to Canterbury and murdered the Archbishop in his own cathedral. It was 29 December 1170.

It has often been said that 'although Thomas did not really live like a saint, he died like one' – with great courage and dignity, commending his cause to God.

The news of the Archbishop's murder spread like wildfire and was received with shock, unbelief and outrage. Thomas became overnight Britain's most popular saint, and in 1173 he was canonized. Miracles began to be recorded at his tomb, and 'The Pilgrims' Way' (immortalized by Chaucer in his *Canterbury Tales*), beginning in London or Winchester, and ending at Thomas's shrine in Canterbury, quickly became the most popular pilgrimage. Meanwhile in 1174 King Henry II did public penance, and the cathedral, having been desecrated by the murder, was re-consecrated.

The story of Thomas Becket is instructive in relation to the struggle between church and state. Neither the King nor the Archbishop was an extremist. The king had no desire to suppress entirely the freedom of the church. Nor did the Archbishop desire to deny the throne its due rights. Nor would one wish to recommend a 'Constantinian compromise' in which the state would favour the church on condition that the church accommodated to it. But would it really have been impossible to develop a 'partnership' in which church and state recognized and encouraged each other's distinct God-given responsibilities in a spirit of constructive collaboration?[3]

Thomas and Henry were clearly both men of strong principle, Thomas being determined to defend the rights of the church, and Henry the rights of the throne. Each resented interference by the other. Each saw himself as the champion of justice. One cannot help admiring their conviction, their courage, and their willingness to suffer for their cause.

But at the same time, behind their principles lay their personalities. According to one biographer 'Thomas was proud, irascible, violent and impetuous, and remained so all his life'.[4] And much the same could have been said about King Henry II. How far then, one is obliged to ask, were their principles influenced by their personalities? How mixed were their motives? How much of their intransigence was due to injured vanity, which made even the smallest compromise unthinkable?

**Becket memorial windows at St David's Cathedral, Pembrokeshire, West Wales.**

136

**Chough on Ramsey Island, Pembrokeshire, West Wales.**

The veneration of Thomas Becket as Archbishop, saint and martyr reached extraordinary proportions. During the decade following his death no fewer than ten biographies were written, while at least eighty ancient English churches were dedicated to him. Many European cathedrals were proud to have a Becket chapel. And one of them was St David's Cathedral in Pembrokeshire.

It is now, therefore, that we return to West Wales. Its Becket Chapel, situated off the cathedral's North transept, and dedicated to St Thomas, was built in 1220 (fifty years after the murder). It was also restored in 1958, when a new stained glass window was fitted, depicting the Archbishop's martyrdom.

I first visited the Becket Chapel in St David's Cathedral shortly after its restoration and, on entering it, I was immediately struck by the prominent display of Becket's simple coat of arms consisting of three Choughs. In heraldic language his escutcheon was 'a shield argent (silver), three Cornish Choughs sable (black), wings expanded, beaked and legged gules (red)'.

So now I am ready to return to the questions with which I began this chapter. What has Canterbury to do with West Wales? My first answer is that a famous twelfth century Archbishop of Canterbury is commemorated in the Becket Chapel in St David's Cathedral. My second answer – in one word – is 'Choughs', for this rare, red-legged crow, which figures on Becket's arms, flourishes along the coast of West Wales.

But why did Becket have Choughs on his arms? For no Chough has been seen in Canterbury or on the Kent coast within living memory. Indeed, as T. A. Coward began his article on Choughs, 'a melancholy interest surrounds the Chough . . . ; it is a species that is going under'.[5] True, the Chough used to be plentiful enough on the coast of Cornwall to be called 'the Cornish Chough'; the legend persists that instead of dying King Arthur turned into a Chough and still haunts the Cornish cliffs; and a Chough perches on top of Cornwall's coat of arms. But the last confirmed report of a Chough in Cornwall was as far back as 1947. We may be thankful, therefore, that plans are afoot to reintroduce Choughs to Cornwall by releasing some birds bred in captivity.

So if there are no Choughs in Cornwall, and no Choughs in Kent, where are they? In Britain their main haunts are the west coasts of Scotland, Ireland and Wales, while their close cousin the Yellow-billed Chough is an inland mountainous species to be found in the Pyrenees, the Alps, the Atlas mountains and across Central Asia to China.

As for West Wales, they are most often to be seen on the Pembrokeshire coast. From several censuses we learn that there were thirty-six pairs during the first half of the twentieth century, forty-six pairs in 1971, fifty-one pairs in 1982 and fifty-eight pairs in 1992.[6] For myself, along the stretch of Pembrokeshire coast I know best, I see them virtually every day, usually in small parties of up to twenty. My red letter day was 22 February 2001, when I saw and watched a flock of about thirty-five.

Back to Becket. We can only assume that centuries ago[7] Choughs not only occurred on the coast of Kent, but were so abundant there that they could be regarded as distinctive to Kent and therefore as appropriate emblems of Canterbury and of its Archbishop. In consequence, Choughs have been preserved on their arms, even though they are absent from their cliffs.

An alternative suggestion arises from the claim that 'beckit' was an ancient name for the chough, on account of its flamboyant beak. Then the play on Thomas Becket's name becomes obvious, for 'the opportunity of a pun was never ignored by medieval heralds'.[8]

It would be hard to exaggerate what Canterbury has lost. To begin with, Choughs are the most handsome of all the crow family, with their livery of glossy black body and scarlet bill and legs. In addition, they are constantly putting on a dramatic aerial performance. They rise and soar effortlessly on the cliff air currents, and then close their wings and dive, swoop or tumble with complete abandon to sea level, only just escaping in time, then wheeling up again and sometimes turning over on their back like Ravens. On the ground, especially on grazing pasture where they feed, probing deeply in the turf for insects, grubs and beetles, they walk, run and hop with equal ease. And all the while, whether on land or in the air, they keep calling to each other with their wild high-pitched *chee-ow.*

I salute them as the spectacular acrobats of the sea cliffs, and compliment Becket on his choice of escutcheon.

FOOTNOTES

1. See the entry in *The Oxford Dictionary of Saints*, edited by David Hugh Farmer (OUP, 4th ed. 1997), p. 472.

2. *Butler's Lives of the Saints*, revised by Kathleen Jones (Burns and Oates, 2000), p. 225.

3. That the apostles Paul and Peter seem to have envisaged this is indicated by Romans 13:1-6; 1 Tim. 2:1-7 and 1 Pet. 2:13-17.

4. *Butler's Lives of the Saints*, p. 225.

5. *The Birds of the British Isles* (1920), Vol. I, p. 6.

6. From the entry on Choughs in *The Birds of Pembrokeshire* by Jack Donovan and Graham Rees (Dyfed Wildlife Trust, 1994).

7. D.A.L: Owen, however, in his doctoral dissertation on 'Factors Affecting the Distribution of the Chough in Britain', mentions that Choughs were nesting on the cliffs of Dover up to the middle or late 17th century.

8. A private communication from Dr C.E.A. Cheesman, Rouge Dragon Pursuivant, The College of Arms, 3 January 2002.

# Epilogue

**'Twilight and evening bell, and after that the night' (Tennyson).**

In this circular tour, round the world in eighty years, we have made sixteen stops and become acquainted with seventeen people. They have been very different from one another: men and women, from the recent and the distant past, African, Asian, European and American, lay people and clergy, Roman Catholic, Lutheran, Reformed and Anglican, explorers in the Arctic and the Antarctic, bishops and evangelists, missionaries, scholars, authors, doctors and martyrs.

But all of them have been either committed followers of Jesus Christ or had come under his influence and inspiration. Each of them also has had something to teach us, and I trust that their lessons have enriched our lives.

# Index

**PHOTOGRAPH ACKNOWLEDGMENTS**

*All photographs by the author, unless otherwise indicated.*

Rev Richard Bewes: p. 49

Billy Graham Evangelistic
   Association: p. 116

Bridgeman Art Library, by permission
   of York City Art Gallery, North
   Yorkshire, UK: p. 32

Mrs Bjørn Bue: p. 16

Tim Dowley: pp. 17, 34 top, 37 top,
   44 bottom, 46, 58, 63 overall

Mary Evans Picture Library: p. 129

P. J. Haalan: pp. 21, 22 top

Illustrated London News: pp. 56 left,
   75 bottom, 108

Image Select International: pp. 131,
   134 bottom

International Nepal Fellowship:
   pp. 64 bottom, 67 bottom

Overseas Missionary Fellowship:
   pp. 77, 78

Moody Bible Institute: pp. 115, 118,
   119

National Portrait Gallery, London:
   pp. 122, 125 top

Natural History Photographic
   Agency: pp. 13 top, 137

Dr Paul Negrut: pp. 28 top, 30

Faith Pocock: p. 83

Release International: pp. 24, 26

SAMS: pp. 100, 104, 105, 107

Sally Tyler: pp. 74 bottom, 75 top

Mrs Ruth White: pp. 82, 85

Corey Widmer: pp. 1, 8, 9

Peter Wyart: 38, 42 bottom, 44 top,
   57, 62 left, 92, 117 bottom, 132,
   133

" We may find a few
or maybe just one or two
Who speak the language of our heart
and give us courage.
These are our guides. "
                    Henri Nouwen,
        " The only Necessary Thing "
                              P. 134

Thank you